THE HOBBIT

A Journey into Maturity

TWAYNE'S MASTERWORK STUDIES

Robert Lecker, General Editor

Demo

THE HOBBIT

A Journey into Maturity

William H. Green

TWAYNE PUBLISHERS • NEW YORK
Maxwell Macmillan Canada • Toronto
Maxwell Macmillan International • New York Oxford Singapore Sydney

Twayne's Masterwork Studies No. 149

The Hobbit: A Journey into Maturity
William H. Green

Twayne Publishers   Maxwell Macmillan Canada, Inc.
Macmillan Publishing Company   1200 Eglinton Avenue East
866 Third Avenue   Suite 200
New York, New York 10022   Don Mills, Ontario M3C 3N1

Library of Congress Cataloging-in-Publication Data

Green, William H. (William Howard)
   The Hobbit : a journey into maturity / William H. Green.
      p. cm.—(Twayne's masterworks studies; MWS 149)
   Includes bibliographical references and index.
   ISBN 0-8057-8806-9—ISBN 0-8057-8807-7 (pbk.)
   1. Tolkien, J. R. R. (John Ronald Reuel), 1893–1973. Technique. 2. Fantastic fic-
tion, English—History and criticism. 3. Middle Earth (Imaginary place) I. Title. II.
Series.
PR6039.032H6 1994
823'.912—dc20   94-12813
                                                                         CIP
                                                                          AC

10 9 8 7 6 5 4 3 2 1

Printed in the United States of America.

Contents

Note on the References and Acknowledgments

The edition of *The Hobbit* used throughout, unless otherwise noted, is the 1966 third edition published in Boston by Houghton Mifflin, which has incorporated in later printings corrections included in the 1978 British fourth edition published by George Allen and Unwin. This is a high-quality illustrated paperback, but the same text (with different pagination) is available from the same publishers in deluxe hardbound editions with additional illustrations. Ballantine Books publishes the text in a smaller format.

The illustrations of "Beorn's Hall," "Lake Town," "The Front Gate," and "The Hall at Bag-End" are from *The Hobbit* by J. R. R. Tolkien. Copyright © 1966 by J. R. R. Tolkien. Reprinted by permission of Houghton Mifflin Co. and HarperCollins Publishers. All rights reserved.

This study culminates a process that began with my 1969 dissertation, supervised by Thomas A. Kirby and typed and proofed by my wife Katherine Sobba Green, who has since supported all my scholarly and creative efforts as she has pursued her own. I am indebted to Jean Dugas for help in formatting the structural table. Francelia Butler of *Children's Literature* and Juliet Knowles, my department head at Troy State University, must share credit for developing my interest in children's fiction as a field—a development that began with my interest in *The Hobbit* in and for itself.

. The Front Gate .

Chronology: J. R. R. Tolkien's Life and Works

1891   Mabel Suffield travels to Africa to marry Arthur Tolkien, English manager of a bank in Orange Free State, in Bloemfontein.

1892   Their first son, John Ronald Reuel Tolkien, called Ronald, born, 3 January.

1894   A second son, Hillary Arthur Reuel, born.

1895   Mabel and her sons return to England, partly for reason of Ronald's health, live with Suffields in Birmingham.

1896   Arthur Tolkien dies of rheumatic fever in Africa. Mabel moves her sons to a cottage in the hamlet of Sarehole, a mile outside the city. She begins to teach Ronald Latin and art, the beginning of four years he later called "the longest seeming and most formative part of my life."

1897   Queen Victoria celebrates her Diamond Jubilee.

1900   Mabel and her sons become Catholic. Her family withdraws financial support, forcing her to live on a small inheritance. Mabel moves to a house in Birmingham, a suburb of Moseley. Ronald Tolkien enters King Edward's School.

1901   She moves again, to a villa behind King's Heath Station.

1902   She moves again, to a suburb of Edgbaston. Tolkien changes schools, enrolls at St. Philip's Grammar School.

1903   Tolkien is back at King Edward's, on scholarship.

1904   That April, Mabel is hospitalized, diagnosed with diabetes. She retires, under sponsorship of Father Francis Morgan, to a rural cottage at Rednal, Worcestershire. The boys join her in June. In November she dies. Father Morgan is designated the boys' guardian.

1905	Tolkien and brother live with Aunt Beatrice, an unhappy arrangement.
ca. 1906–11	Tolkien privately studies Old English, Old Norse, and Gothic, begins to invent languages with their own grammars and histories, and writes poems, some in invented languages.
1908	The brothers board with a Mrs. Faulkner on Duchess Road. Edith Bratt, also an orphan, is there.
1909	That autumn Father Morgan discovers the romance between Ronald and Edith, which he fears may lead to early marriage and ruin Tolkien's career prospects. Tolkien fails to win an Oxford scholarship.
1910	Father Morgan moves the boys. Ronald is forbidden to contact Edith until he is twenty-one. She leaves Birmingham. Ronald speaks Gothic and Old English in a school debate. He is awarded a small scholarship to study classical languages at Exeter College, Oxford.
1911	During the summer, he enjoys fellowship of clique of like-minded students at King Edward's, the Tea Club. He hikes through mountains in Switzerland. He enters Oxford.
1912	Begins study of comparative philology under Joseph Wright, joins and camps with a cavalry regiment, reads a paper on the *Kalevala* (a Finnish mythological epic), writes poems.
1913	Turns twenty-one, contacts Edith Bratt. She breaks engagement to another man. He takes a Second Class in exams and transfers from classics to English, with emphasis in philology, and formally studies Old Norse.
1914	Edith becomes Catholic, and they are formally engaged. Britain declares war on Germany. Tolkien decides to complete his degree before serving.
1915	Receives First Honors on final examination, takes a commission, and begins army training. Continues to write poetry in "fairy language" and English, including the anthologized "Goblin Feet."
1916	Marries Edith. Shipped to France, where he serves as battalion signaling officer in the Somme. Survives horrors of mechanized war, is sent home in November with trench fever.
1917	Convalescing, begins *The Book of Lost Tales,* including "The Fall of Gondolin," and spends most of the year hospitalized. Son John is born.
1918	Posted in Staffordshire, continues writing *Lost Tales.* When

the war ends, joins the staff of the *New English Dictionary* (later know as the *Oxford English Dictionary*) at Oxford and works in the letter "w."

1920   Appointed Reader in English Language at Leeds University. Second son, Michael, is born.

1922   Publishes *A Middle English Vocabulary*. E. V. Gordon hired at Leeds, and they begin work on their standard edition of *Sir Gawain and the Green Knight*.

1924   Appointed Professor of English Language at Leeds. Third son, Christopher, is born.

1925   The *Gawain* edition is published. (By now he has published various poems and reviews as well.) Elected Rawlinson and Bosworth Professor of Anglo-Saxon at Oxford.

1926   Forms "The Coalbiters," a faculty club reading Old Norse. Meets C. S. Lewis.

1928   This summer scribbles first sentence of *The Hobbit* on a blank examination book page and begins to tell the story to his children.

1929   Daughter, Priscilla, is born.

ca. 1930   Completes full draft of *The Silmarillion* (printed in *The Shaping of Middle-Earth*, 1986). Begins scribbled draft of *The Hobbit*, completed through the death of Smaug.

1932   C. S. Lewis reads a manuscript of *The Hobbit*. Tolkien at work on an expanded *Silmarillion* and continues to publish poems and articles.

1934   Receives two-year Leverhulme Research Fellowship.

1936   Delivers lecture, "Beowulf: The Monsters and the Critics," before British Academy. Susan Dagnall, with Allen and Unwin, reads *Hobbit* manuscript and suggests that he complete it. He does. It is accepted for publication.

1937   *The Hobbit,* published in autumn, is a commercial and critical success. Stanley Unwin asks for a sequel. Tolkien submits *Father Christmas Letters* and *The Silmarillion*. They are rejected. In December, writes first chapter of "New Hobbit," which will become *The Lord of the Rings*.

1938   Expands *Farmer Giles of Ham* manuscript to book length. *The Hobbit* published in the United States by Houghton Mifflin and receives *New York Herald Tribune* award as best children's book of the season. Drafts twelve chapters of *The Lord of the Rings*.

1939	Lectures "On Fairy-Stories" at St. Andrew's University. World War II begins. Sixteen chapters of the sequel written.
1940	"Prefatory Remarks" to John R. Clark Hall translation of *Beowulf* published.
1942	Stocks of *The Hobbit* burned in a London air raid.
1943	Son Christopher enters the Air Force.
1944	Tolkien writes long letters to Christopher, who is serving in South Africa, and sends him new chapters of *The Lord of the Rings,* now into book 5.
1945	"Leaf by Niggle" is published in the *Dublin Review.* Germany is defeated. Atomic bombs are dropped on Japan. Tolkien elected Merton Professor of English Language and Literature and says he is putting *The Lord of the Rings* "before all else."
1947	Notes discrepancies between *The Hobbit* and its sequel, particularly as to the nature of the ring.
1948	Summer, *The Lord of the Rings* is completed.
1949	*Farmer Giles of Ham* published.
1950	Negotiates with Collins, a London publisher, to publish *The Silmarillion* along with the hobbit sequel. *Farmer Giles* sells slowly.
1951	Revised edition of *The Hobbit* published.
1952	Collins returns manuscripts. Tolkien agrees to allow Allen and Unwin to publish *The Lord of the Rings* without *Silmarillion.*
1954	First two volumes of *The Lord of the Rings* published.
1955	The last volume, with appendices, published.
1957	*The Hobbit* is published in German translation.
1959	Tolkien retires from his Oxford professorship.
1960	*The Hobbit* is published in Polish.
1962	Poems, *The Adventures of Tom Bombadil,* are published. *The Hobbit* is published in Portuguese and Swedish. Tolkien's edition of the Middle English *Ancrene Wisse* is published.
1964	*Tree and Leaf* is published.
1965	An unauthorized Ace paperback edition of *The Lord of the Rings,* the first inexpensive version, triggers sudden popularity of Tolkien on college campuses and attention from the press. There is a legal conflict over publishing rights. An authorized revised edition issued by Ballantine is a best-seller. Tolkien Society of America is founded.

1966	A revised third edition of *The Hobbit* is published.
1967	*Smith of Wooton Major* is published.
1968	The Tolkiens move to Poole, near Bournemouth, in a seaside resort area.
1970	The staff of the *Oxford English Dictionary* compiles an entry for "hobbit."
1971	Edith Tolkien dies, aged eighty-two.
1972	Tolkien returns to Oxford, with rooms at Merton College. Receives honorary doctorate from Oxford University and is honored by the Queen.
1973	Visiting friends in Bournemouth, becomes ill and dies a few days later, on 2 September, at eighty-one years of age. His son Christopher, as literary executor, is left to complete *The Silmarillion*.

LITERARY AND HISTORICAL CONTEXT

Demo

1

Historical Context

J. R. R. Tolkien's early life was a succession of bereavements that created in him a deep nostalgia for the past. Born in South Africa in 1892, the son of an English bank manager, Arthur Tolkien, he was taken to England with his mother and younger brother when he was only three, ostensibly to visit relatives. The next year, after Arthur's death, the little family moved to an unspoiled hamlet just outside Birmingham, where Mabel Tolkien taught her sons Latin, German, and art. Tolkien recalled his four years there as "the longest-seeming and most formative part of my life."[1]

But when he was eight the idyl suddenly ended. His mother converted to Roman Catholicism and lost the support of her Protestant family. She moved the boys into the city, where Tolkien entered school. In the next three years the family moved twice more, and then Mabel Tolkien died after a summer of convalescence in a rural cottage that reawoke in her son memories of a lost Eden. The cause was diabetes, but Tolkien saw his mother as a martyr to her faith.[2] He and his brother, Hillary Arthur Reuel, were boarded in a succession of private houses, wards of a stern but charitable priest, Father Morgan, whom Tolkien loved, feared, and admired.

From his teens Tolkien obsessively studied medieval language and myth, inventing grammars and mastering subjects years above his grade level. Though haunted by depression, he developed strong friendships at his all-male school and went on to Oxford as a scholarship student and aspiring poet. At first majoring in Latin and Greek, he later found his calling in the history and early literature of English and was near graduation when World War I broke out—a war in which he witnessed the horrors of mechanized combat. This reinforced his feeling that terrible powers were loose in the world. Though Eden, he remembered, was possible, and God, he believed, was provident, he saw his century as a dark age, a century that had ceased to believe in good and evil and had lost its grip on the healing power of myth. Barely twenty, he resolved to invent the necessary myths for his beloved England.

Marrying young, to Edith Bratt, perhaps the only woman after his mother he had ever loved, Tolkien lived an intense double life. On the one hand was the public professor, first at Leeds, then at Oxford. In this public role he was a hard-working teacher and scholar who made important contributions to the study of medieval language and literature, a conservative academic husband and father concerned about the family income and his children's health. But behind this facade was the fantasy poet, an obsessive midnight embroiderer of unfashionable tales in prose and verse about elves, dragons, and lost kingdoms.

Though his fantasies did not become famous until the 1950s, Tolkien had been working and reworking epic prototypes of them, writing to please himself, for some forty years by that time. The mythic tales of Tolkien the wounded medievalist—written at first with little hope of reward in his own struggle with the symbols of healing and salvation—have, of course, become classics. But these tales might never have escaped his desk drawer had not one of them, a bedtime story for his children, lent a fairy-tale friendliness to his invented world. *The Hobbit* began Tolkien's career as popular writer and became the basis for all that followed.

In the first half of the twentieth century an adult story about elves and dragons could not be taken seriously; fairy tales were nurs-

ery stories, beneath adult attention. Even the science fiction of H. G.
Wells and his successors huddled under a mantle of scientific prediction; and the pure fantasies of Lord Dunsany and James Branch Cabell
succeeded only as witty entertainments, like detective stories. For
more than a century, realism of one kind or another had dominated
adult fiction, so long that the realistic bias was no longer to be seen as
a temporary fashion. To be taken seriously, modern stories had generally to be set in actual places and times, preferably recent ones, to
reflect real social structures, and to be strictly governed by probability.

By the 1930s, when *The Hobbit* was written, the newest fiction
was experimental and unrealistic in its way. The work of Franz Kafka,
James Joyce, and William Faulkner, for instance, stretched the boundaries of traditional realism to create a revolutionary modernism. But
though these works broke free of the old dramatic realism, they only
intensified psychological realism and embraced decadence. Aberrations
and fantasies were usually situated in the minds, often unhealthy ones,
of characters in realistic settings. Readers of the Nightown chapter in
Joyce's *Ulysses* knew the material brain, the social setting, in which it
was fantasized: the fantasy was a disease framed in a realistic skull.
And if a fantasy was presented unframed, as by Kafka and the French
surrealists, it was, Tolkien noted with distaste, tinged with morbidity,
like visions of a mind disturbed by fever.[3] This morbidity, so unlike the
wholesome clarity of fairy tales, was seen by critics in the century of
Sigmund Freud as a mark of artistic seriousness.

A work of serious modern fiction was also expected to be
morally realistic: good and evil were not to be polarized and clarified
by the author but were to imitate the blurred values of real human
experience. Though authors obviously created their characters, told us
all we knew about them, modern authors were expected to avoid
telling us that characters were good or evil—indeed to avoid dramatiz-
ing clear moral polarities. The goal was complexity, and in the early
years of his popularity Tolkien was often accused of lacking "moral
complexity," as if that lack were itself an evil. If a modern author took
moral sides, he was expected to use winks and camera angles, sharing
points with both teams—not, like the author of *Beowulf*, describe one
character as "good," another as a "devil." Even works with realistic

settings and probable events might be "escapist" if they articulated good and evil too clearly, and especially if good triumphed in the end.

As a medievalist, Tolkien saw most of these critical biases not as universals but as diseases of modern thought. And luckily they did not apply to children's fiction. It was considered correct, even obligatory, to moralize when writing for the young; and children's "primitive" minds were supposed to be receptive to fantasy and to demand simple explanations. The juvenile loophole was the reason that Tolkien published his first book of fiction for children, unable to find an adult audience for the morally serious myths he had already written, the archaic, densely written fairy epics he began in 1917 as *The Book of Lost Tales*. He asserted in 1957 that he had written fairy stories not because of an interest in addressing children, "but because I wish to write this kind of story and no other" (*Letters*, 297).

Fortunately, there was ample precedent in children's publishing for the kind that Tolkien wished to write. In addition to the popular fairy story collections of the Grimm Brothers and of Andrew Lang, he acknowledged the influence of George MacDonald's *The Princess and the Goblin* (1872), of the medieval romances of William Morris, of S. R. Crockett's *The Black Douglas,* and especially of a neglected children's fantasy by E. A. Wyke Smith called *The Marvellous Land of Snergs* (1927). He mentioned with familiarity many others, including *Alice's Adventures in Wonderland* (1865), *The Wind in the Willows* (1908), *Brer Rabbit* (1906), *The Time Machine* (1895), and *Treasure Island* (1883). And other classics prepared the way for *The Hobbit*—if not as influences, then as precedents in the minds of readers. Some of the most important may be the scientific romances of Jules Verne, H. Rider Haggard's treks into the unknown (especially *King Solomon's Mines* [1885], which shares dozens of motifs with *The Hobbit*), and E. Nesbit's scholarly fantasy *The Story of the Amulet* (1905). Even L. Frank Baum's *The Wizard of Oz* (1900), too vulgarly American for Tolkien, lurks behind the acknowledged influence of Wyke Smith's fantasy. As a children's book *The Hobbit* grew in well-tilled soil.

Here Tolkien discovered an accepted modern form, the boy's adventure tale, through which he could share with a large audience the myths of sacrifice and wholeness—Christian values interfused with the pagan myths of northern Europe—which he had discovered in *Beowulf* and *Sir Gawain and the Green Knight.* It is no accident that *The Hobbit* appeared at about the same time as Professor Tolkien's two great works of literary criticism, *Beowulf: The Monsters and the Critics* and "On Fairy-Stories," for they are all about the same business. They set out to restore a heritage that he believed the literature of his century had sadly lost.

2

The Importance of the Work

The Hobbit is important as a suspenseful and original story synthesizing existing material in an utterly new way to support an archetypal theme. It is the flagship of all of Tolkien's popular writing. His adult masterpiece, *The Lord of the Rings,* was planned as a sequel, a second "hobbit book," and grew magnificently out of control. The hobbit books imprinted college student culture in the 1960s and became models and inspirations for a revival of heroic fantasy, a vast expanse of postmodern fiction that Tolkien still rules.

The Hobbit is a variation on the archetypal story of apprenticeship in which an inexperienced hero goes out into the world and discovers himself through adventures and hardships. *Tom Jones* and *Treasure Island* are classic examples of the pattern—as old as the stories of Joseph in Genesis and Telemachus in *The Odyssey*—a staple of fairy tale, romance, and popular fiction.

Typically the protagonist of these tales is young, of course, but Tolkien manages an interesting variation: his hero is a middle-aged gentleman who has stayed too close to home and become spiritually stagnant. Like the heroes of Hesse's *Steppenwolf,* Goethe's *Faust,* and Cervantes's *Don Quixote,* Bilbo is some fifty years old when he answers a call to step from his womblike home into a magical otherness. This is normally not material for juvenile fiction, this dangerous flight from second childhood, but Tolkien makes it work by inventing a diminutive hero who has avoided worldly experience. Not only is Bilbo small, but boyishly open and aimless, much like a good-natured adolescent whose parents are on extended vacation. No reference is made to ravages of age in Bilbo (wrinkles or loss of stamina), and he is much younger than the long-lived, bearded dwarves he accompanies. So, by omission and contrast, Tolkien achieves indirectly what Goethe must use the machinery of a witch's potion to achieve in *Faust:* he creates a male-menopausal protagonist endowed with the energy and appeal of youth, a children's-book hero.

In this juvenile masterpiece that hides, like a Trojan horse, an adult story, Tolkien reinvents traditional heroism for his century. The myths of northern Europe and the old heroic poetry he loved were composed within a military aristocracy, where the bravado of Beowulf and Sigurd made sense. With the postmedieval rise of the middle class, the emergence of merchants and artisans as the patrons of books, the type of the aristocratic swordsman grew more and more remote; and the twentieth century nearly lost belief in traditional heroes, substituting antiheroes, superheroes, and doomed victims. Tolkien skillfully wove motifs from medieval myth into *The Hobbit* (*Letters,* 22) to explore and demonstrate how a hero who is timid, bourgeois, and ethically Christian might achieve at his own level feats comparable to Beowulf's. The book is a narrative position paper in the debate between nihilistic relativism and traditional values. Monsters still exist: fighter bombers, if not dragons; bigots, if not goblins. Moral good and evil exist, and heroism is still needed. However inexperienced and small we are, like Bilbo we can show courage and make a difference.

Such idealism struck a resonance with students in the 1960s. As much as Tolkien disagreed with "hippies" about drugs and sex, Bilbo's message of idealistic simplicity and hope—the ultimate triumph of young courage against the dragons of a corrupt establishment—spoke to the generation that protested racism, fascism, pollution, and war. Bilbo's "sit-in" on a dragon's doorstep, putting himself at its mercy until he found its weak spot and forced an uncorrupted remnant of the establishment to act, seemed a practical model for social reform, at least in the years before the Kent State massacre. And somewhere between Bilbo's hole by the Water and the elvish community at Rivendell, young adults found paradigms for their communes and universities. By the end of the decade, Tolkien was unofficial required reading for American college students,[1] and his books were bestsellers. In 1972, Tolkien discovered that the "main business" of his British publisher was marketing his fiction. Sales of his thirty-five-year-old children's book were "rocketing up to hitherto unreached heights" (*Letters*, 421).

Admittedly, campus graffiti read "Frodo Lives," not "Bilbo Lives." *The Lord of the Rings* and its hero, Frodo, were the focus of attention. But Bilbo's meeting with Gandalf at the door of his hobbit hole is the historical moment when the Oxford professor's dubious hobby, previously shared only with friends and in a few public readings, burst out of his desk drawer and into the literary world. Had *The Hobbit* not successfully penetrated the juvenile-fiction chink in his era's antifantastic armor, Tolkien would never have begun the trilogy that possessed the imagination of a decade and, along with the magical realism of Gabriel García Márquez, trumpeted the death of modern realism.

The Hobbit is, as Randel Helms has demonstrated, *The Lord of the Rings* "writ small,"[2] the prototype for all that followed. Writing it, Tolkien discovered harmonious relationships between several existing literary genres that happy coincidence threw together in his life: medieval narratives, fairy tales, classic children's fiction, and popular adventure stories. Tolkien's emulation of "escapist" fiction, particularly late-Victorian boys' books, explains hostile reactions from critics such as the high-modernist Edmund Wilson, who called Tolkien's work "juvenile trash," and medievalist Burton Raffel, who marginalized it as not "literature."[3] But the success of the Middle-earth books depended on Tolkien's discovery that serious themes and heroic motifs could be popularized by orchestrating them in the "escapist" mode represented by Alexandre Dumas, Jules Verne, Edgar Rice Burroughs, and H. Rider Haggard.[4] It was while writing *The Hobbit* that Tolkien made this discovery and a major postmodern movement began, though its promise was not to be recognized for almost half a century.

3

Critical Reception

Published in Great Britain on 21 September 1937, *The Hobbit* sold so well that a new printing was needed before Christmas. The presence of positive reviews was assured by Tolkien's close friend C. S. Lewis, who in early October published anonymous raves in the *Times Literary Supplement* and in the *Times* itself, influential publishing addresses. Lewis called attention to the "deft" scholarship behind the story, its appropriateness for a wide range of ages, and its bringing together good things "never before united." He predicted that *The Hobbit* would become a classic. Though one anonymous review in *Junior Bookshelf* found Bilbo's adventures "contrived," nearly all the early reviewers, British and American, displayed enthusiasm that forecast a place on juvenile booklists.

Though Tolkien began *The Hobbit* for the amusement of his children, he denied that it was especially intended for young readers.[1] Of course, early reviews were typically buried in columns bothering over illustrations and age suitability, back alleys unlikely to attract an adult audience, so it was not until the eruption of Tolkien fandom in the 1960s that Bilbo's quest attracted many adult readers. Still, early reviewers noticed a potentially wide age appeal. A review published in

11

New York twelve days before the American release asserts that "if the book does not please American children, so much the worse for them."[2] And C. S. Lewis had already asserted that, though *The Hobbit* will amuse younger readers, only adults reading it repeatedly "will begin to realize what deft scholarship and profound reflection have gone to make everything in it so ripe, so friendly, and in its own way so true."[3] It is no hollow sales slogan that the story appeals to "all ages."

Richard Hughes, a perceptive early critic, identified what Tolkien called "the Richard Hughes snag": the likelihood that he would overshoot his young audience if he wrote any more about hobbits (as, of course, he did overshoot them). Hughes, in a letter to the publisher, called *The Hobbit* "one of the best stories for children I have come across for a very long time" but also mentioned the "snag"—that parents might find some parts "too terrifying for bedside reading" (*Letters,* 23). In his published review, confined under the heading, "Books for Pre-Adults," Hughes noticed the difficulty of assigning a book's appeal to a specific age group—a point Tolkien acknowledged a year later in his Andrew Lang lecture, "On Fairy-Stories," where he disputed the idea that fairy stories were particularly suited for children. Hughes notes that Tolkien is "so saturated in his life-study that it waters his imagination with living springs." *The Hobbit* is "Nordic mythology" rewritten by a man so intimate with it that he does not merely rearrange, but "contributes to it first hand."[4] In April 1938 the book won a *New York Herald Tribune* cash prize as best juvenile story of the season.

In the seventeen years between publication of *The Hobbit* and the renewed interest provoked by its sequel, the book remained in print in England and America. It secured early and without controversy a niche it occupies today in histories of children's literature. In his two histories of children's books in Britain, Marcus Crouch sets the highest literary standards—books must be good books first, for children second—and lavishes unmixed praise on *The Hobbit* as "an exciting story of adventure, a tragedy with comic episodes, a picaresque romance with strands of magic in it, an historical novel about the remote past which, by the author's craft, becomes more real than the present. . . . By any standard, [it] is a great book."[5] Crouch's 1972 history observes that Tolkien's original achievement has been blurred by the *Lord of the Rings* "cult" and praises *The Hobbit* as a different sort of success from its sequel, less apparently allegorical, more about character development than good and evil, more friendly and humorous, yet "a story of high adventure, with vividly imagined episodes, funny, grotesque, sad and noble, all sustained and given continuity by the writer's scholarship and his command of every detail of his created world."[6] I have cited Crouch for his evocative style, but *The Hobbit*'s rank as classic children's book is uncontested. Comparable praise appears in Judith Saltman's *Riverside Anthology of Children's Literature* and in Zena Sutherland and May Hill Arbuthnot's *Children and Books*—virtually anywhere juveniles are surveyed.

Critical reception has been less consistent in the field of Tolkien studies, where critics are obliged, sometimes grudgingly, to read *The Hobbit* as the first of a four-volume set, overture to *The Lord of the Rings.* Here Bilbo sits in the shadow of Frodo and is occasionally seen in a dim light, particularly by those who dislike the paraphernalia of classic children's fiction: cute verses, clarified good and evil, and asides to small readers. We read, as it were, sitting in Papa Tolkien's tobacco-scented lap, and some find that lap uncomfortable. A strong instance is Paul H. Kocher, whose analysis of *The Lord of the Rings* is perceptive and enthusiastic but whose response to *The Hobbit* is to argue circular proofs that the children's book is more childish than the adult one. His avowed purpose is to reassure would-be readers of *The Lord of the Rings* that they don't have to "tackle" *The Hobbit* first—a work that "often puzzles, sometimes repels outright."[7] Fans of Bilbo might say the same thing about Kocher's humorless complaints.

Typically, however, major critical treatments of Tolkien's fiction have given *The Hobbit* respectful attention as precursor of the trilogy, usually devoting a chapter to it as prelude. Early reviews by insiders such as C. S. Lewis and W. H. Auden set the tone for criticism that analyzed Tolkien's work as folklore and myth, with particular attention to the quest and to the obvious echoes of medieval literature and Victorian medievalism. Later came serious analysis in terms of depth psychology, twentieth-century popular fiction, and philology. Most long studies of Tolkien have some value for a student of *The Hobbit,* but many assume that children's books are inferior books, the attitude that inspired Francelia Butler to subtitle her first issue of *Children's Literature* "The Great Excluded." Typically, the adult story is the "masterpiece," and students of children's literature must gather the crumbs that fall from its table.

Robley Evans's 1972 *J. R. R. Tolkien,* ignoring publication history, treats *The Hobbit* as part of a unified four-volume story. Though this does reflect Tolkien's later wish—his revisionist 1950s harmony of Middle-earth—the approach imports into Bilbo's story ideas absent from the 1937 edition and scarcely hinted at even in late revisions. Bilbo's ring, for instance, has none of the cosmic power that it absorbs as it passes to Frodo in the sequel. It is a minor bit of magical technology, symbolic perhaps, but irrelevant to the Necromancer's power over Middle-earth. Evans's discussion of the One Ring, moving freely in and out of *The Hobbit,* imposes a 1950s spin on the 1937 story. His perspective is from within *The Lord of the Rings,* and when distinctions are made, the sequel is supreme. Bilbo's quest, says Evans, "does not prepare the reader for the scale of the action and the paradoxical delight . . . which expand the range of Tolkien's major work and give it power over its readers."[8]

Randel Helms's 1974 *Tolkien's World,* the best early book about Tolkien, maintains the distinction between original and sequel—indeed clarifies it—in two chapters devoted to *The Hobbit.* The first demonstrates that the sequel is structurally a repetition, the same plot expanded and elaborated. As an event in Tolkien's career, the 1937 volume is celebrated and enhanced by Helms's approach. *The Hobbit* is one of literature's "pivotal moments" when "a gifted writer rediscovers a decayed or discredited form and then creates an audience for it" (Helms, 1). In the compass of a children's book, Tolkien "discovered his theme, learned what he had to say and how the fairy story could say it" (Helms, 20). In the second chapter, "The Hobbit as Swain," Helms launches a jaunty but insightful psychological interpretation of Bilbo's maturation in terms of Freud and Erich Neumann, then runs abruptly aground—as if he can no longer abide reading a children's book psychosexually. His reading, he declares, has been "parody," though its points are valid. The problem is that "Tolkien's children's story deserves little serious, purely literary criticism" (Helms, 52). Again, a juvenile is a juvenile.

Many other critics have seen *The Hobbit* as a symbolic story of growing up, a basic theme in children's fiction. The second chapter of my own 1969 dissertation, printed a decade later in *Children's Literature* as "The Four-Part Structure of Bilbo's Education," examines the hobbit's progress toward "full moral development" as a spiraling sequence of episodes ending at "Homely Houses."[9] A similar thesis is developed in explicitly Jungian terms by Dorothy Matthews in her 1975 article, "The Psychological Journey of Bilbo Baggins,"[10] and most subsequent discussions of the book mention Bilbo's maturation, at least in passing.

The Hobbit gets respect but little useful interpretation in Anne C. Petty's 1979 folklore study, *One Ring to Bind Them All: Tolkien's Mythology.* Petty's approach is structuralist, her thesis being that Tolkien appeals to readers because he follows universal patterns of the folktale as identified by Joseph Campbell, Claude Lévi-Strauss, and Vladimir Propp. Tolkien's fiction brings the quest myth to fulfillment, rather than ending with the fragmentation typical of most recent myth-based fiction; thus it validates traditional forms. "Any serious study of the fictive world of Tolkien," Petty says, "must cast a discerning eye upon the original tale of the hobbits as an interesting and necessary prelude."[11] *The Hobbit* is treated as a marginal work, a nutcracker for *The Lord of the Rings,* and even it is secondary to a folkloristic thesis. Petty's work yields a mathematical proof of morphological correctness but few critical insights.

More useful is Timothy R. O'Neill's 1979 Jungian analysis, *The Individuated Hobbit.* O'Neill attempts the impossible, in 166 pages to explain the theories of C. G. Jung and apply them to five volumes of mythic fiction; so the results are at worst thin, at best selective. Nevertheless, the book is a good preface to a labyrinthine subject. O'Neill's reading of *The Hobbit* focuses on three episodes, leaping over clusters of chapters as if they did not exist, but he does take the book seriously and interprets it as an effective myth of maturation. A lengthy analysis of Beorn, the bear-man in the story, "in the general category of Self symbols because of his symbolic hermaphrodism"[12] is

O'Neill's fullest insight into the psychological implications of Bilbo's adventure.

Richard Mathews's 1978 paperback, *Lightning from a Clear Sky,* includes a full section appreciating *The Hobbit* through plot summary mingled with comments on sources, symbols, themes, and structure. Mathews needed a fact-checker. For instance, his numerological interpretation assumes, "the total number of chapters in the story is 21"[13] (the number is nineteen), but his reading is usually on target. He questions Helms's belief that the children's book does not deserve literary criticism: "Whatever the particular age group, the mythic achievement as well as the successful style are literary elements worthy of praise" (Mathews, 12). And then he argues for the artistic coherence of Bilbo's adventure, using Helms's insight into the importance of "renunciation" in Tolkien's fiction, the way Bilbo and others gradually learn to be heroically unselfish.

Jane Chance Nitzsche's 1979 *Tolkien's Art* approaches Tolkien with a focused methodology. A medievalist, she uses Tolkien's nonfiction to construct a proof that "his creative works reflect his interest in Medieval English literature, especially Old English."[14] Though she believes *The Lord of the Rings* transforms medieval ideas "into art more successfully—and subtly," she finds medieval themes to be clearer in *The Hobbit* (Nitzsche, 3), which she too defends against Helms's charge that it is "merely" children's literature (Nitzsche, 31). One defense of Tolkien's art, a controversial one, interprets the adult narrator as a fictional character, a successful foil for the nobler and more sympathetic Bilbo. A medieval parallel here is Chaucer's Pilgrim, the foolish character the great poet gave himself in his own wise poems. Nitzsche goes further than many readers would (and neglects the narrator's function as "chorus") by assigning a harsh list of traits to Tolkien the Narrator, calling him a "monster" (alongside Smaug) in "Tolkien the Author's Art" (Nitzsche, 46–48).

If Nitzsche's insights are sometimes forced by her self-imposed focus on the medieval, yet she reads *The Hobbit* with high analytical seriousness, and her results suggest unexpected depths in the story. She discusses the medieval conception of the sinful king as monster and analyzes the progression of monsters in the story as an exploration of all the seven deadly sins, moving from the lower bodily sins to the higher spiritual ones. She divides the story into two parts and finds a Dantelike pattern of sins, monsters, and false kings in each. A contrast of various kings under the mountain leads her to characterize Bilbo as an Augustinian hero who has defeated love of self and achieved moderation. A peevish middle-aged man, she points out in a brilliant paradox, "grows up" to become a joyful child (Nitzsche, 45). In Nitzsche's analysis, *The Hobbit* is a wise and profound book, driven by theological and moral insights.

In contrast to chapters that either attack the story as juvenile or defend it as fit for adults, Lois R. Kuznets's 1981 "Tolkien and the Rhetoric of Childhood" analyzes *The Hobbit* as a contribution to "the great tradition of the British children's classic." In her view, the book's excellence as a juvenile is the chief reason it deserves attention.[15] Using *Alice's Adventures in Wonderland, The Princess and the Goblin,* and *The Wind in the Willows* as touchstones, Kuznets lists a catalog of traditional traits: the obtrusive narrator, characters appealing to preadolescents, maturation within a short time span, dialogue and verse, circumscribed geography, and concern with safety or danger. Traits that earlier critics have called weaknesses become strengths within this tradition. The obtrusive narrator, Kuznets finds, is skillful at maintaining a thematic focus. She praises Bilbo as an androgynous childlike hero who appeals to both boys and girls in elementary school, the period of sexual latency. His incremental self-integration and "basic sanity" are held up to admiration, not twisted into wounded saintliness as Frodo's character is in *The Lord of the Rings*. "Bilbo lives. And Bilbo joins Alice, Curdie, Rat, and Toad in the gallery of such sane and down-to-earth protagonists" (Kuznets, 160–61).

Katharyn F. Crabbe's reading of *The Hobbit* in her 1981 *J. R. R. Tolkien* is at first condescending, then generous. The book, she says, though successful, is "neither complex nor ambitious" and "far less interesting and much less an artistic achievement" than its adult sequel.[16] After anatomizing the juvenile style with its "avuncular asides" (a bright turn of phrase), Crabbe concedes that the book is still worthy of critical attention: "Like other fairy tales, *The Hobbit* is thematically concerned with the human situation, not simply with childish ones" (Crabbe, 31). Then she lavishes, page for page, four times as much space on the story as she does on its adult sequel. It is possible to list only some of her points. She compares fairy tale and myth to describe *The Hobbit* as a fairy tale. She finds a meaningful progression in the sequence of cave descents. She interprets the ring and sword as gender symbols, the hero as androgynous. She compares Bilbo as "low mimetic" hero with "high mimetic" heroes traditional in adventure tales. And she parses the themes of limited heroism, of good versus evil. Crabbe reads the story chiefly in its own terms, with little overt theoretical appeal, and demonstrates the complexity and effect of Tolkien's art.

The Hobbit catches scattered comments in two books produced by Robert Giddings, who (together with Elizabeth Holland) leads a movement of irreverent readings of Tolkien as escape novelist, naive conservative, sexual neurotic, class spokesman, crypto-pagan, and so forth.[17] All the articles in Giddings's 1983 anthology have in common serious (often negative) rereading outside academic traditions. Probably Giddings's clearest insight is that Tolkien's fiction is modeled on popular adventure novels, such as John Buchan's *The Thirty-Nine Steps* and Rider Haggard's *King Solomon's Mines,* which Tolkien preferred over modern "literary" novels. Here is an obvious explanation for his popularity, more persuasive than folktale morphology and medieval motifs. Kenneth McLeish's 1983 essay calls *The Lord of the Rings* "the rippingest yarn of all," an Edwardian allegory quilted from bits of traditional children's and adult popular fiction—then offhandedly praises *The Hobbit* as Tolkien's "masterpiece, because it never aspires to allegorical significance, and is therefore superbly self-consistent."[18]

"No Sex Please—We're Hobbits: The Construction of Female Sexuality in *The Lord of the Rings,*" Brenda Partridge's essay in the same Giddings anthology, examines the tender physical bond between Frodo and Sam, the love story of the trilogy, and links it to sexual ambiguity and fear of women's sexuality in C. S. Lewis, Tolkien's close friend. Partridge's consistent homoerotic reading of Tolkien's sexual symbolism demonstrates why he and Lewis, who expressed strictly Victorian views of sexual morality, disliked psychological readings.

Squarely in the academic mainstream, T. A. Shippey's 1983 *The Road to Middle-Earth* is the definitive study of Tolkien's literary sources and the way his academic field shaped his fiction. Shippey worked closely with Humphrey Carpenter, Tolkien's authorized biographer, and with Christopher Tolkien to produce a study of grace, authority, and substance. Throughout, Shippey assumes the serious worth of *The Hobbit*. When he explains how Tolkien created "asterisk-worlds" from language history, his insights apply to Bilbo's story; and his chapter about *The Hobbit* makes new critical points as it gleams with erudition. He characterizes Bilbo's magic ring (not Frodo's) as an "equalizer" like Colt's revolver, making success possible but still demanding heroism.[19] He describes the smug narrator's frequent "of course" as a device to inspire belief and "create a sense that more information exists round the edges of the story, and that events are going according to rules just hinted at, but rules just the same" (57). Shippey eradicates all doubt that Tolkien the storyteller was informed by Tolkien the scholar and removes any reasonable suspicion that the juvenile book is child's play.

Since the long-awaited 1977 publication of *The Silmarillion* and subsequent publication of stories and fragments from the private papers, emphasis in Tolkien studies has necessarily shifted away from *The Hobbit* and *The Lord of the Rings*. The excitement of new ground to break is elsewhere—with the elves of the First Age. For instance, in the two volumes of *The Book of Lost Tales* (1983–84), we read directly about the goblin wars and the fall of Gondolin often mentioned in *The Hobbit*. The volumes of new material make Bilbo's adventure a smaller piece of a larger mosaic, but a piece of unquestionable importance, a point of origin. As high-quality children's fiction the book's status is uncontested, and many adult critics have discovered in it workmanship worthy of serious study and comment, both in the framework of Tolkien's other work and as a free-standing story.

4

A Theory of Fairy Stories

In Defense of Fantasy

An important background for reading *The Hobbit* is Tolkien's 1939 lecture "On Fairy-Stories." The lecture expresses a crucial point in his career. A year and a half before, *The Hobbit* had been published and was so successful that, a few days before Christmas of 1937, Tolkien had begun to write a sequel. His principal motive was probably financial. His publisher, Stanley Unwin, had assured him that a second "hobbit book" would sell. As Oxford professor, Tolkien held a social station higher than his income and had for years worked summers and holidays grading examinations from regional and overseas colleges to support his growing family. So the role of successful children's author seemed an attractive alternative, though it too interfered with his scholarly work.

Through the first part of 1938, the forty-six-year-old professor tried to double as novelist and scholar, but the load associated with his research fellowship was crushing. He wrote his publisher: "With three works in Middle English and Old English going to or through the press, and another in Old Norse in a series of which I am editor under my hand on behalf of the author who is abroad, and students coming in July from Belgium and Canada to work under my direction, I cannot see any loophole for months" (*Letters,* 36). That August his physician ordered him to rest, and relaxing into the congenial role of storyteller, Tolkien completed the first eleven chapters of his new hobbit book by October. The sequel to *The Hobbit* seemed well begun. Then the story stalled, and a frightening realization dawned.

With the equivalent of two hundred printed pages written, he realized that he was still in the expository sections of a work of vast scale, one that would strain his schedule or displace scholarly work for years to come. Moreover, it was a work that offered no guarantee of financial success, even of publication, because it had mutated into an adult fairy story, a noncommercial genre. This was not the series book that the publisher wanted, certainly not a potboiler sequel for children. Was the project worth continuing? With this question weighing on his mind, Tolkien wrote the lecture "On Fairy-Stories," "when *The Lord of the Rings* was beginning to unroll itself and to unfold prospects of labor and exploration as daunting to me as to the hobbits" (*Tree,* vii). The lecture reflects implicitly on the value of *The Hobbit* as Tolkien questions and ultimately affirms the dignity of fairy stories, not as folk artifacts or childish entertainment, but as expressions of a deep contemporary need. Tolkien came to see the fairy story (a term that grew to include all his fantasies and fictions like them) as the century's stepchild and savior. The fairy story was like a scorned third son, the luminous shadow of a dark mechanical age. The twentieth century had neglected the genre because it had lost touch with the human heart and lost faith in a divinely ordained world.

Though biographical facts suggest that the Lang lecture "On Fairy-Stories" was, for Tolkien, the resolution of a weighty midlife question, his style is light, sometimes whimsical, not demanding much from his academic audience. Little about his diction suggests that underneath the public statements he is reassuring himself that he has taken the right turn, that he will not be wasting his life if he devotes his best years to expanding the world of *The Hobbit.* His audience, he knows, is a friendly one, interested in Andrew Lang and fairy stories, but it can hardly be expected to share his evangelical feeling for nursery tales. Much like Chaucer and Dante, Tolkien devises a modest persona through which to speak—a scholar yes, but a scholar awkwardly out of his field—and argues successfully for more than he claims to prove. "Ridiculous though it may be for one so ill-instructed to have an opinion on this critical matter," he begins (*Tree,* 46) and then turns upside-down Samuel Taylor Coleridge's literary theory, which he calls "recent," while modestly choosing not to confront the great critic by name. And, even as dozens of far-flung examples display Tolkien's immense learning, he claims to be no more than a reader who enjoyed fairy stories as a child and has thought about them since. His claims will, in the end, leap to cosmic conclusions, but still he poses as a modest fellow. Like Bilbo, Professor Tolkien is "only quite a little fellow in the wide world after all!" (255).

Under this mantel of modesty, Tolkien's lecture summons benchmark works of literary criticism and corrects points of their theories that are hostile to fantasy. His closest model is Sir Philip Sidney's *Defense of Poesy,* with its idealistic appeals to common sense, its analysis of genres, and its claims for the "golden" world of fantasy as opposed to "brazen" nature.[1] Like Sidney, Tolkien defends writing about imaginary things, but where Sidney defends all fiction against history and philosophy, Tolkien defends fantasy fiction against mainstream realism. It is a smaller field of battle, but the same war. And, of course, Aristotle's *Poetics,* which Sidney claimed as his model, is also behind Tolkien's analysis. Tolkien uses the terms *eucatastrophe* and *recovery* in a pattern that parallels Aristotle's use of *catastrophe* and *catharsis.* An Aristotelian definition of the fairy story implies modestly that tales like *The Hobbit* are as serious as tragedies and equally worthy of critical attention.

The great romantic critic Coleridge, author of the medieval-style "The Rime of the Ancient Mariner," might seem a natural friend of fantasy. Indeed, in I. A. Richards's classic 1934 monograph, *Coleridge on Imagination,* there is much that Tolkien must have found agreeable. Like Coleridge, Tolkien wants to understand the "poetic faith" that allows readers to believe. Like Coleridge, he sees fantasy as a means to liberate readers from stale, habitual perceptions—from a world that has become dead matter: "this elevation of the spirit above the semblances of custom and the senses of a world of spirit, this life in the ideal, even in the supreme and Godlike, which alone merits the name of life, and without which our organic life is but a state of somnambulism."[2]

But the critical theories of Coleridge, gathered from essays, lectures, and letters, had been adopted by I. A. Richards and the emerging "New Critics" into a critical orthodoxy that discouraged fantasy fiction, though it encouraged the fantastic in poetry. "Make-belief is an enervating exercise of fancy," Richards wrote in his 1934 monograph, "not to be confused with imaginative growth" (Richards, 171). Though Richards goes on to praise "greater" mythologies, the Coleridge of 1939 critical orthodoxy had generally been drafted (or misread) into the service of Tolkien's enemies, those for whom there was no good fiction but a realistic one.

To correct this, Tolkien assumes "the powers of Humpty-Dumpty" and redefines Coleridge's central term, *imagination*. Coleridge had defined imagination as the highest creative faculty. Our very intuitive grasp of a coherent world he called *primary imagination,* and any artistic creation that exhibited the same organic coherence, whereby each part is modified by each other part, he called a work of *secondary imagination.* A work of secondary imagination, however fabulous, inspires belief in an audience, or at least "a semblance of truth sufficient to procure for these shadows of imagination that willing suspension of disbelief."[3] Tolkien repeatedly echoes Coleridge's famous phrase, "willing suspension of disbelief," arguing that it misrepresents the kind of belief that successful fantasies inspire. And Tolkien sees no point in using imagination to describe coherent artistic creations and using fancy (a debased form of fantasy) to describe incoherent ones. Making a philologist's appeal to word derivation, he switches the terms, substituting *fantasy* for Coleridge's *imagination.* According to Tolkien, *fantasy* should refer to coherent artistic creation, *imagination* to the mere making of images. This reversal of terms undermines Coleridge's authority, already lost to the armies of realism, but leaves the machinery of his theory available to justify serious fantasies such as *The Hobbit.*

As he openly switches terms, Tolkien quietly assumes a more traditional set of assumptions about the world. Coleridge's worldview is subjective, based on the German idealism of Kant. His primary imagination is the "living Power and prime Agent of all Human Perception." It may be a "repetition" of the creative I AM (Richards, 57), but it is not the creative word itself, nor is it the natural world of the senses either. For the idealist, the things we see are in large measure projections of our minds. Things are not really "out there," not as we see them anyway.

In contrast, Tolkien's worldview is objectivist, compatible with the orthodox Catholic thought of Thomas Aquinas. Tolkien assumes a creator God and an externally real perceived world: God made the intelligible world for us to see and understand, and it is real. Our perception is, of course, limited and sometimes distorting, but that does not compromise the reality of the objects that we see. When human beings see as we were "meant to," God is showing us his world. So Tolkien's "primary" element is commonsense reality, which he calls the *primary world.* Our natural belief in this reality Tolkien calls *primary belief.* Secondary belief is a different quality of belief, belief that we provisionally grant to works of art, such as a fairy story, because they have "the inner consistency of reality" (*Tree,* 47).

Tolkien generates a full set of terms to track the process of creation and belief. A successful fantasist uses art to *subcreate* a *secondary world* that earns our secondary belief by having an "inner consistency" like the primary world. A good fantasy is a successful "repetition" (Coleridge's term works here) of the rational creative Word of God. Thus the subcreator of a secondary world is the creator god of that world, but is a contingent or limited god. Tolkien and the concrete details of his fictional world—Beorn, Wargs, goblins, and giant spiders—remain framed in the primary world of 1930s England, God's world, where Tolkien is himself a creation lent the power to create: "we make still," he wrote, "by the law in which we're made" (*Tree,* 54). As we read about Tolkien's secondary world, we are ourselves framed in our own historically later primary worlds. Always, if we are sane, we know where we are. Always, the secondary world remains secondary, and belief in it remains secondary belief.

We accept the world of a fairy story not because we confuse it with the primary world; that would be insane, and if it happened often, the worst charges hurled against fantasy would stick. Tolkien's stories would degenerate into neopaganism or demon worship, things he certainly abhorred. But, in fact, secondary belief coexists with a healthy primary disbelief. As we read *The Hobbit,* for instance, we continue to disbelieve in dragons and magic rings in the world of our own experience. Primary disbelief need not be "suspended," even momentarily, for us to derive the full effect of Bilbo's adventures. Indeed, the special appeal of fantasy would be lost if we actually did suspend disbelief. If I believed that kissed frogs became handsome princes, the tale of the frog-prince would be ruined for me. I would lose the force of its magical absurdity (*Tree,* 56–57). The desirable effects of fantasy depend on a mood of strangeness.

In the Lang lecture Tolkien names three main benefits of the fairy story: recovery, escape, and consolation. Recovery results from a fusion of the strange and commonplace that characterizes subcreation. A close encounter with goblins in the Misty Mountains allows us to return to our own kindred world and see through the clouds of habit that normally obscure our view of "things as we are (or were) meant to see them" (*Tree,* 57). Anyone who has returned home after a long trip understands the force of recovery, the sudden revision of homely things in their new context; and fantasy helps us to see clearly, not just our homes, but the whole primary world. "It was in fairy-stories," says Tolkien, "that I first divined the potency of the words, and the wonder of the things, such as stone, and wood, and iron; tree and grass; house and fire; bread and wind" (*Tree,* 59). Magical realism and fantasy, two fictional modes that have become fashionable since the 1960s, offer what Tolkien calls recovery, renewal of natural sight that adults as well as children may need in our increasingly artificial age.

By naming escape as a second "benefit" of fairy stories, Tolkien confronts the usual accusation that fantasy is "escapist." Fantasy does provide escape, he acknowledges, from the soulless "realities" of a mechanized and materialistic age: escape from power poles into forests, from electric light into lightning, from railway stations to a blue sky. But this, he argues, is the admirable escape of a prisoner into freedom (*Tree,* 60). Tolkien's medieval education, Catholic religion, and romantic conservatism all show here, but we need not share these views to see his basic argument. The escape offered by a fairy story is escape from the transitory into the enduring: lightning may persist eons after electric lights have evolved or vanished, and the sky has already outlasted most urban railway sheds.

Through fantasy we escape into elemental things that have constituted human experience for centuries and will for centuries to come. Beyond these obvious material escapes, we may also escape into ourselves and rediscover ageless desires of the human heart. Airplanes are unique to our brief age, but human beings have always longed for "the noiseless, gracious, economical flight of a bird" (*Tree,* 66). From the roots of this longing we enjoy (sitting safe with our book) Bilbo's flights with the eagles. And, of course, all have desired the great escape that only fairy stories can promise us (and here Tolkien anticipates his characterization of the Christian gospel as a fairy story that is true), escape from death (*Tree,* 67–68). Much that is fabulous in *The Hobbit* is not sorcery but the natural magic of a subcreated world—a world governed by subtly altered laws that allow us to escape our limitations and satisfy timeless desires.

Finally, triumphantly, fairy stories offer the consolation of the happy ending. Just as the *catastrophe,* the change from good to bad fortune, is the basis of Aristotle's famous definition of tragedy, so the *eucatastrophe,* the sudden joyous turn, is the basis of Tolkien's definition of the fairy story. Just as Aristotle defined tragedy by its effect, which was pity and fear, so Tolkien defines the fairy story by its effect, which is joy. A fairy story succeeds insofar as it evokes this joy (*Tree,* 68–69). Tolkien wrote in 1944 that he knew he had written a "story of worth" when he reread *The Hobbit* and felt the joy of the *eucatastrophe* as Bilbo looked up in the midst of a losing battle and exclaimed, "The Eagles are coming" (*Letters,* 101). The Consolation produced by this joy in the face of danger is the residual effect of the fairy story, just as *catharsis* is for Aristotle the residual effect of tragedy. Fairy stories infuse us with strength to live in hope.

CONSTRUCTING A TALE OF TALES

The arrival of the eagles may be the ultimate *eucatastrophe* in Bilbo's story, but the story is driven by a series of other seemingly hopeless cliff-hangers followed by sudden joyous turns. If this elemental level were the only level, then *The Hobbit* would be episodic, little more than an anthology of fairy stories strung in chronological order like pearls on a necklace. Edith Nesbit's otherwise brilliant subcreations, *Five Children and It* and *The Story of the Amulet,* suffer from this kind of discontinuity, perhaps because they were written as magazine serials. What distinguishes Tolkien's fantasy from these less successful ones, which are so much like it in page-for-page texture? *The Hobbit* has narrative momentum: it pulls readers steadily toward the final happy ending. It has, in Aristotle's terms, unity of action. Its first chapter projects a problem that is not resolved until the end, and every chapter between moves noticeably toward that resolution. But such unity, however important, is only a static frame, a structural harness in which the episodes pull as a team. The energy comes from the episodes themselves, from well-paced alternations of tension and relaxation through credible dangers and sudden joyous turns.

The fairy story, the basic structural unit of *The Hobbit,* is a short form. The obligatory joyous turns console us at frequent intervals, typically once per chapter, within a longer narrative based on the fairy story form. But these alternations of peril and rescue must not steal interest from the great joyous turn that grandly resolves the whole story. The parts must not upstage the whole. Upstaging of the whole by the parts is what happens in, for instance, Edgar Allen Poe's powerfully written fantasy, *The Narrative of Arthur Gordon Pym,* with its gripping episodes and puzzling ending. Though better written, realized in more grim detail than almost any comparable story—certainly better written than the successful novels of Jules Verne and Edgar Rice Burroughs—Poe's book fails because his genius and critical theory do not address the demands of larger unity. In the end readers are left with nothing but scattered effects.

Poe, we may recall, is the critical theorist who said that all poems are short (like the basic unit of the fairy story) and that "What we term a long poem is, in fact, merely a succession of brief ones—that is to say, of brief poetical effects."[4] *What we term a long fairy story* (he might equally have said) *is, in fact, merely a succession of brief ones— that is to say, of brief eucatastrophic effects.* But Tolkien clearly understands that fear of a final great catastrophe and the distant promise of ultimate rescue must permeate the succession of lesser tales. *The Hobbit* has unity of action, most obviously, because through all of the adventures in Wilderland and beyond, its readers have heard of Smaug the Dragon and are waiting, like Bilbo, to meet him. But Tolkien's narrative is more than a linear sequence of tales with a goal in view.

One way of approaching the unity of the story is to visualize a "tree diagram," the system of branching lines used to chart classification systems, sentence grammars, or family descent. The whole of the story is divided into parts, and those parts are also divided into parts, with each larger or smaller part built around the *eucatastrophic* structure of the fairy story. In the overall story of *The Hobbit,* which is itself resolved by the sudden arrival of the eagles at the Battle of Five Armies, there are five parts, each consisting of several chapters and resolved by its own sudden joyous turn—and then an interval of rest at a place that may be called a "Homely House." Inside each of these parts, the constituent chapters typically contain subtales built on the *eucatastrophic* pattern of the fairy story. As the chapters support the parts, so the parts support the greater story, linking them all into a working whole. The tree diagram is the harness in which the chapters pull as a team.

Accurate as the tree diagram may be, it is too flat to capture the organic connectedness of the episodes, the way they build toward a single effect. A better figure is the ascending spiral, the figure of progress through recapitulation. The spiral is the form expressed in orchestral music when a small ensemble begins a piece by stating a theme and then repeats the underlying theme with variations throughout, but with constantly evolving tone colors until the originally simple theme is transfigured in a crescendo of the whole orchestra. Finally, there may be an unassuming coda recalling the beginning. This common orchestral pattern is executed with authority in Tolkien's book, where each tale contains many parts equivalent to parts in other tales, and these parts function as symbols (though always within a credible story) of the hobbit Everyman's maturation and self-discovery. Each *eucatastrophe,* with each pattern of events leading up to it, is commentary on every other one, building toward a climax of theme that coincides with the climax of action.

The pattern of the spiral, of cumulative restatement, is a common property of most long quest stories in which the heroes grow, from *The Divine Comedy* to *Treasure Island,* from *Captain Marvel* to *Star Wars.* And Tolkien is certainly not original in building a story around a series of cliff-hangers and narrow escapes. These are the staples of popular escapist fiction, including a mass of pulp writing that is altogether ephemeral and shallow. What is original is Tolkien's discovery (a discovery he made writing *The Hobbit* as a children's book) that such fiction could be a serious genre to serve high and ancient purposes, that it could express patterns for living and become for our age what the ancient myths were for theirs, even—if only in a secondary way—what the Christian gospels were for theirs. The spiraling pattern of perils and escapes that seduces us into reading drivel can also inspire us to rediscover our humanity in a dark world where goblin dictators rule capitols and dragon airships dwarf the fire-drakes of old. The consolation of the fairy story, though not explicitly Christian, is nourishment for the human soul: it is "*evangelium,* giving a fleeting glimpse of Joy, Joy beyond the walls of the world, poignant as grief" (*Tree,* 68).

Through his writing of *The Hobbit* as a children's book and his first steps toward a sequel, Tolkien discovered a common ground where ancient storytelling rituals overlapped with popular fiction, a high hill from which a Christian medievalist passionately out of step with the secular mythology of his age could address an audience of millions. In his Andrew Lang lecture, "On Fairy-Stories," he formalized and reaffirmed that discovery, then turned back to the work for which he is most famous, remythologizing modern life in a subcreated world of hobbits.

5

A Psychology of Dragon Slayers

An important theory applicable to fantasy stories was developed by the great Swiss psychologist C. G. Jung (1875–1961). Though Tolkien wrote his defense of fantasy independently of Jung's theory, the two men shared a belief in the healing power of myth, and Jung's ideas illuminate the complex psychological implications of Tolkien's stories.

Originally a follower of Sigmund Freud, Jung founded his own school of psychological analysis on parallels he noticed between his patients' dreams and the mythologies of ancient and primitive cultures. Jung noticed repeated patterns in dreams, stories, and pictures from a wide range of cultures and times and called these repeated patterns *archetypes*. Because archetypes appear in such a wide range of unconnected materials, Jung deduced that they were images of the basic structures of the human mind. As a scientist, Jung understood that a given presentation of an archetype by a given analyst was tentative, colored by the conditions of the analysis. No particular image of mother (much less any particular mother) actually is the mother-archetype, but one underlying archetype is understood to affect all human perceptions of real mothers and of many other things—such as dragons, caves, houses, bags, and bears—which on the surface may not seem motherly.

Because of Jung's scientific attitude toward the subject he pioneered, his own writings are often more like narratives of a search than reports of results. In the works of his students, however, we find his theory summarized in final form and extensively applied to stories that resemble *The Hobbit*. Erich Neumann (1905–60) discusses the dragon-slaying hero as a symbol of increasing consciousness and freedom from the mother in two great scholarly studies: *The Origins and History of Consciousness* (1954) and *The Great Mother: An Analysis of the Archetype* (1955). Later, in a series of four volumes beginning with her 1970 *An Introduction to the Interpretation of Fairytales* (volumes that were the models for Robert Bly's 1990 best-seller *Iron John*), Marie-Louise Von Franz analyzes fairy stories in detail for archetypes of maturation. An important contributor to Jungian theory, Von Franz demonstrates how profound themes can be expressed in apparently simple traditional stories.

Jungian interpretation uses a number of key terms. To begin with, the whole mental process (which Jung calls the *psyche*) is divided into two parts, the *conscious* and the *unconscious*. The conscious part includes what we know about: intentions, memories, and the ego. The *ego* is what we mean when we say "I," the self-aware pilot of the body. Everything else, whatever its origins, is unconscious. This includes not only archetypal tendencies we share with the rest of humanity but lost memories, unquestioned habits, and implicit assumptions about culture or language. We spend much of our time sleepwalking through actions determined by the attitudes of groups of people around us, a robotic process Jung called *mystical participation*. Most mental processes are unconscious.

But the unconscious contains unacceptable and contradictory impulses. It is the business of the early decades of life to construct a conscious ego and to bury in the unconscious any aspects of the psyche not consistent with it. Males disown feminine traits. Thinkers reject feeling. Honest people bury their natural will to lie. We repress aspects of the psyche and deny them even as we act on them. Besides the ego, each of us constructs a number of simplified, masklike personalities, or *personas,* for use in social situations. Routine social contacts and success in a profession require that we create suitable dramatic roles and stick to them.

The problem with the personality fragments called ego and persona is that, necessary as they are, they are not the whole psyche; discarded and unrealized parts continue to exist and unconsciously affect thought and action. The buried parts have their own proper energy: if they are not expressed, a person falls into neurosis, particularly in the later years of life. Managing the flow of energy is a more-or-less unconscious center that reflects and influences all the rest, even parts that the ego rejects and denies. This transcendent center Jung calls the *self.* The self is not the "I," but the center of a much greater wholeness. The self is an unconscious archetype, represented indirectly through symbols, and experiences of the self are often associated with the supernatural.

The self exists at birth. The newborn psyche is all unconscious self, a little god at one with a tiny universe. A child first achieves ego-consciousness by realizing that the body of the caretaker ("mother," regardless of biological connection) is a separate thing. At this point, the infantile ego splits off from the self, leaving most of the psyche in its original unconscious state, profoundly identified with the primal mother. But the pattern and purpose of life, says Jung, is to achieve psychic wholeness by raising large portions of the self into consciousness and developing a secure and flexible ego that cooperates with the self, mediating between it and the world. The goal of human life is this state of wholeness that Jung called *individuation,* a state that can also be called maturity. The self, the buried center of the psyche, directs the ego/hero on a perilous quest toward consciousness that, according to Jung, has been expressed for millennia in the search for lost treasure, often associated with killing a dragon.

The archetypes of the *shadow* and the *anima* participate in the quest. The shadow, or dark side, is a figure representing traits rejected by the ego. The shadow includes dangerous traits that clearly must be rejected, but it also includes useful powers—such as intellect in a physical person or physical force in an intellectual—that were discarded to define the ego. Often the dark side has powers the ego desperately needs. A shadow lesson in lying, for instance, is needed by an ego that wounds friends and makes enemies with careless words. And even destructive shadow traits need to be acknowledged as unacted impulses. A gracious understanding that evil exists inside ourselves, not just in other people and the world, is an important early step toward individuation.

Next, the hero typically meets the contrasexual self, a buried identity represented by a person of the opposite sex. In traditional tales the ego is usually represented by a masculine hero, and, once he has accepted his shadow, the self may show to him a feminine face, a princess, his anima. In *The Hobbit,* a story completely lacking female characters, we may look for the anima in symbolic forms. Associated with the anima and forming a bridge between it and the self are archetypal feminine symbols such as the ring, the egg, the jewel, and the mountain.

Through encounters with shadow and anima, the hero establishes contact between the conscious ego and the hidden self. Throughout this process, however, the ego risks being devoured or possessed by one of the archetypal personalities. He may identify with the persona and become an empty social shell. He may become his shadow, as Dr. Jekyll did, with obvious bad effects. He may be possessed by the feminine, the Great Mother: an archetype that is evil when it devours or enslaves—good only as it protects, nurtures, and releases. Finally, he may identify with the self. Rather than simply interacting with the god-like self, he may imagine that his conscious identity is somehow identical with it and become inflated with its power. Possessed by the self, he falls into infantile selfishness and becomes an compulsive monster.

The goal of life, expressed in terms of the dragon slayer's quest, is to discover the self, the treasure guarded by the mother. This is individuation, wholeness. But it must be the culmination of a process, a completed quest. Premature closure with a symbol of the self, seizing on that symbol as the "precious" while one is still under the domination of the persona, shadow, or anima, can destroy the hero.

Jung developed his theory by comparing the struggles of his patients with the images and structures of traditional tales. The correspondences that he and his students found help us to see the healing and instructive effects of traditional stories, particularly of Tolkien's stories, which are modeled freely on tradition and guided by his own half-conscious impulses. Jung's theories translate fairy stories into the scientific language of psychology.

Demo

A READING

Demo

6

An Adventure of Self-Discovery

MR. BAGGINS OF BAG-END

The Hobbit begins with three pages in the author's voice introducing us to Bilbo Baggins, a well-to-do bachelor from a family of conservative hobbits. Hobbits, by the way, are a fictional branch of humanity, not a mythical species (*Letters*, 158). Their definitive traits of hairy feet, sharp senses, and small stature, as well as their conservatism and common sense, may occur in people today. Bilbo's quiet strength, his point of view close to the ground, and his vulnerability among "big people" echo universal facts of childhood and speak to adults who feel small in the world of global media.

Though Bilbo may remind us of Winnie-the-Pooh with his frequent daydreams of food, his nearest counterpart in A. A. Milne's stories is Piglet, always fearful because he is a Small Animal, yet rising to heroism and generosity beyond his size. For instance, Piglet allows himself to be raised by a string on a rescue mission out of Owl's fallen house, and he donates his own house "in a sort of a dream" to the homeless Owl.[1] Milne's tiny hero inspires the longest and grandest "Hum" from Pooh, the poetic Bear of Very Little Brain (seven whole verses), and is cheered to discover in Pooh's naive parody of heroic song that he, Piglet, is brave (Milne, 290–91). Such a comic textual hero Bilbo Baggins becomes—a hero who repeatedly models his action on stories and ends up writing the story of his own adventures, humorously titled "A Hobbit's Holiday" (254). Even Piglet's pride in his imaginary grandfather "Trespassers William" (Milne, 16) parallels Bilbo's pride in "Old Took's great-grand-uncle Bullroarer, who was so huge (for a hobbit) that he could ride a horse" (24). Like Piglet, Bilbo is a comic figure who must assert himself bravely to earn an identity in a world where he is almost beneath notice, even among undersized companions.

At first, Bilbo is a generic hobbit. In the first two paragraphs he is called simply "a hobbit" as attention is given to his comfortable underground home like the furnished holes of Mole and Rat in *The Wind in the Willows*. Tolkien begins in a fanciful world reminiscent of Grahame, Milne, and Carroll, with more attention to setting than to character and no hint of heroism. In the third paragraph we learn that our hobbit is a Baggins, member of a wealthy family that is respected "because they never had any adventures or did anything unexpected" (11).

Finally, deep in the fourth long paragraph, a rambling discussion of Bilbo's mother and hobbits in general, Tolkien offhandedly drops Bilbo's name—a short name in a long sentence characterizing his mother's people, the Tooks. Clearly, though he has prominent family connections, Bilbo is not a prominent person. Like a child, he is defined as an offshoot of his family, his "house." He is undifferentiated, absorbed (the terms here are Jung's) in mystical participation with the hobbit community. Bilbo behaves "like a second edition of his solid and comfortable father" (12). He has not found himself. When the action finally begins three pages into the book, we understand that Bilbo is a late bloomer, a middle-aged child whose identity is submerged in generic hobbitness and shaped by his dead father's heritage.

This may not seem bad. Certainly, Bilbo appears to live a stable life and enjoy creature comforts, and there is no obvious surface

The Hall at Bag-End, Residence of
B. Baggins Esquire

reason why he could not live like a happy child until he dies. Nevertheless, the wizard's benign intervention and a great deal of psychological theory suggest that Bilbo's nervous passivity may read as depression. Something like the miserable little underground creature Gollum may be festering at the roots of his personality, in the early stages of transforming him into a bitter little Scrooge. In fact, Bilbo is in no danger of becoming a cannibal like Gollum but of becoming like his grasping, materialistic cousins, the Sackville-Bagginses, who personify Baggins traits in negative purity at the end of the book. Marie-Louise von Franz puts the case forcefully when she refers to the "human psychological fact . . . that evil entails being swept away by one-sidedness, by only *one single* pattern of behavior."[2]

Between his paternal and maternal families, the conservative Bagginses and the adventurous Tooks, Bilbo is suffering an unrecognized crisis because he has lost the Tookish half of his character. His life is aimless and stagnant because of his one-sided habit of avoiding risks. Because he has shut off the Took half of himself, the Baggins half has become a sterile reenactment of the dead paternal past. Ironically, Bilbo has also reenacted the choice of his mother, who lost her Took name to become a Baggins. Perhaps for her this was a rash decision, an adventure, but for Bilbo it is a passive birthright. He is his father and his mother but not himself. The elder Baggins at least married an exotic woman, had a son, and built a home; but Bilbo has only slept, eaten, kept house, and taken walks. In fifty years he has accomplished nothing worth mention. When a wizard appears at his doorstep to give him what he "asked for" (15), the hobbit is arguably at a crossroads, destined either to wither and die or to break into new life.

A HERO'S VOCATION

Bilbo's situation can be compared to that of Don Quixote, another stagnant fifty-year-old who embarks suddenly on an adventure. But Bilbo's departure, unlike the Don's, is a sane act, however mad it seems to the neighbors. Clearly, though he parallels Don Quixote, Bilbo is also much like Sancho Panza, the sensible peasant whom Don Quixote drafts as his "squire." Bilbo combines in a single not-yet-integrated whole the foolhardy gentleman and the practical bumpkin: the dreamer of adventures and the "solid and comfortable" Baggins. Loosely speaking, Don Quixote is a Took, Sancho Panza a Baggins, and Bilbo is both. Physically, of course, he resembles the short, pot-bellied peasant, and like Sancho, he is insular and naive, fond of food and comfort. Repeatedly during his adventure, more than a dozen times, Bilbo is said to long for food and home, like Sancho mourning over the empty wine bottle.[3] Unlike Don Quixote, Bilbo thinks about creature comforts. His concern over going off to fight a dragon without his handkerchiefs contrasts with the Don's forgetting to pack money and clean shirts (Cervantes, 42).

But a more important contrast is the fact that Bilbo's call to adventure comes from a compelling authority outside himself, from a quixotic wizard who summons him suddenly to discover his buried potential. Sancho, an unschooled peasant, accepts his call to adventure because it comes from an educated gentleman, and Bilbo receives his call from an even higher authority. In *The Hobbit*, Gandalf is a legendary wizard, but in Tolkien's later accounts, he is no less than an angel (*Letters*, 202). As orthodox angel, Gandalf has a limited mandate to interfere in human affairs. He can function only as a catalyst to provoke and guide the faithful. He sets events into motion and then must leave them to unfold in accordance with moral character and free will.

As Gandalf's allusion to prophecy on the final page suggests, *The Hobbit* is about a man's discovering his vocation, discovering his true self. Though Bilbo seems at first to be only a literate Sancho, a comic "little fellow bobbing and puffing on the mat" (24), he is "Belladonna Tooks's son" (14), heir to a family acquainted with elves. He is a hero called to change the world. By the end of the story Bilbo is quixotic in the highest sense: he has dared and succeeded beyond all sane expectations. A pot-bellied, middle-aged child has imitated Sigmund and Beowulf, faced a dragon and contrived its death.

Tolkien explains in a later retelling of the story that Gandalf does not transform Bilbo supernaturally. The old wizard merely remembers a young hobbit's "bright eyes, and his love of tales, and his questions about the wide world outside the Shire,"[4] and calls out a heroic inner child, a lost vocation. In *The Hobbit*, as in classical tragedy, character is destiny. Gandalf understands and teases into action Bilbo's latent heroic desires, "dwindled down to a sort of private dream" (*Unfinished*, 337). Tolkien makes his design explicit in a 1966 letter to his publisher: hobbit heroes are "ordained individuals inspired and guided by an Emissary to ends beyond their individual education and enlargement" (*Letters*, 365).

The Hobbit is a fairy story: its world a world where things are broken open alchemically to show what they really are. Inside the half-witted third son of the tale is the future king. Inside the frog is a prince. And inside the selfish little Baggins is a noble Took "more worthy to wear the armour of elf-princes than many that have looked more comely in it" (230).

OPPOSITION AND RETURN

The narrative is not only linear, a story of forward progress, but cyclical. *The Hobbit* begins and ends with a visit from Gandalf, and Bilbo gives his adventures the cyclical title "There and Back Again" (254). Gandalf starts the action by visiting with dwarves, and the action ends with a visit from Gandalf and a dwarf. Pipe smoking, a standard ritual of bonding in the male adventure stories of Jules Verne and Rider Haggard, ceremonially opens and closes the book. Bilbo is on his doorstep smoking a large pipe when Gandalf first appears (13), and at the very end Bilbo laughs and hands the wizard a tobacco-jar (255). In their communal smokes, the men create and compare symbols of completion and repetition, smoke rings.

Northrop Frye's description of the typical "quest romance" fits *The Hobbit* exactly: it "takes on a spiral form, an open circle where the end is the beginning transformed and renewed by the heroic quest."[5] The hobbit has returned at a higher level, and recapitulations within the last scene show this. Bilbo's discovery of his inner heroism, his hand in the death of the dragon, his self-sacrifice—all of this has been productive. His waistcoat is larger and has "real gold buttons," and the dwarf has a longer beard and a magnificent jeweled belt. The folk around the once-desolate Mountain, we are told, have prospered (254–55), and Bilbo has continued his heroic life-style into the less hazardous arena of hobbit social life. He has become a nonconformist—a cosmopolitan, at least in the eyes of his rural neighbors. He has "lost his reputation" and taken to "writing poetry and visiting the elves" (254). In short, he has found himself. Bilbo has become a complete person separate from his benighted community. The final scene of *The Hobbit* is a positive echo of the beginning.

But the beginning of the story is also echoed, however darkly, by Bilbo's encounter with the dragon at the Lonely Mountain. This is the turning point of the book, a terrible parody of home at the place farthest from home, a sort of fun house mirror at the edge of the world. In opposition to the hobbit's round front door under the Hill, where he blows rings of smoke, there is Smaug's round Front Gate under the Mountain, out of which issue smoke and steam (175). To mature, Bilbo must leave his ancestral home, the womblike hobbit-hole, and pass uncorrupted through the tomblike dragon lair, the mountain tomb that becomes the womb of heroic rebirth. This is, by the way, his third dangerous underground journey from east to west, the night sea journey of the archetypal solar hero, and in each case Bilbo must make important parts of the journey alone and in darkness. The hobbit hero must confront and overcome the dragon, a vast incarnation of the infantile state that he has been outgrowing throughout the story.

The two ends of Bilbo's adventure, the hobbit's Hill and the dragon's Mountain, are congruent but opposite and are connected in the text. The action begins with Bilbo standing by his door, and a chapter title identifies the rock shelf that leads into the dragon's lair as "the Doorstep." As Bilbo leaves this doorstep to enter the heart of the Mountain, he wishes that he could "wake up" and be back home in his own front hall (183). The tunnel is, of course, a negative double of his front hall, but he cannot awaken from its dark negativity except by going forward, facing the dragon who is snoring up ahead, sounding like a pot boiling on a fire (184). The reference to a cooking pot establishes a connection, for it echoes the kettle that Bilbo rushes to set on the fire in his own hole when unexpected guests arrive for tea—a grisly doubling, of course, because, when Bilbo arrives as an unexpected guest, he expects to be eaten, not to eat. The importance of the hobbit's decision to face the dragon is emphasized in the text: "Going on from there was the bravest thing he ever did" (184).

Given the connection between Bilbo and Smaug, implicit in the connection between their homes, it is interesting that when the hobbit finds his home (like Smaug's) being plundered, he takes the loss of silver spoons (254) much more gracefully than Smaug takes the loss of the two-handled cup. It is Bilbo's high resistance to greed, a vice Tolkien calls "dragon-sickness," that permits the hobbit to remain "happy to the end of his days" (254). In coming to know himself, he learns how to be happy within his limitations.

A TALE OF TALES

The movement from the Hill to the Mountain and back again, the book-length story, is made up of five parallel parts, five component tales. In each of the five parts Bilbo sets out from a homelike refuge, is opposed by monstrous foes, is saved by a *eucatastrophe* ("a sudden joyous turn"), and then arrives at another homelike refuge. In each component tale he faces the foes in tunnel-like darkness after touching or passing over a body of water. The foes are deadly, but, oddly, they do not immediately kill their victims. Rather, they trap victims in bags or blind tunnels, to starve or be eaten later. Food is the theme sounding constantly under the narrative, like a drone string, the cycle of hunger and gratification. And there is always a lack of good food associated with Bilbo's perils—almost as if as long as there is an ample supply of delicious food, no monsters can come near. The hospitable homes that end each component tale, arrived at after passage over a second body of water, offer resupply of food. In each of these refuges, or Homely Houses, a host sets retrospectively the tone of the component tale, reflects the type of perils that have been overcome, and sets the next component tale into motion.

These parallels are strong, but not monotonous, because of many variations: sometimes perils come in clusters, and the last two tales are melded together by a major shift in point of view and a narrative flashback, which prevents the slackening of narrative tension occasioned by the earlier Homely Houses and drives the story toward its climax. Still, however transformed, the component tales are remarkably parallel in their parts, like seasonal variations on a familiar ritual, an oft-told tale.

Also, in each of the component tales, Bilbo experiences an initiation, enacts progressively a pattern of testing and reward. He is placed in situations where he must choose to act, and when he acts appropriately, he is rewarded with a prize—in all but one part a physical object, and in one part (the third) promotion to a position of leadership of the company that at first only grudgingly accepted him as a follower. When the company is in danger, Bilbo tries within his limited but growing abilities to save it. And in each of the component tales, a

Structural Patterns in *The Hobbit*

Part	Chapters	Foes	Saviors	Places of Peril	Water into Peril	Water out of Peril	Homely House: Host	Prize	Baggings	Night Sea Journeys
I	1-3	Trolls	Gandalf	Dark Under Trees	Bridge at Edge of Wild	Bridge at Rivendell	Rivendell / Elrond	Sword	Troll Bags	•••••
II	4-7	Goblins / Gollum / Wargs	Gandalf / Bilbo / Eagles	Caves / Dark Under Trees	Storm / Underground Lake	Carrock	Beorn's Hall / Beorn	Ring	Chains / Cave Door / Treetops	Under Misty Mountains
III	8-10	Spiders / Elves	Bilbo	Dark Under Trees / Caves	Black Stream	Forest River to Esgaroth	Esgaroth / Town Master	Leadership	Spider Silk / Prison / Barrels	Through Wood-elves' Cave
IV	11-14	Dragon	Bilbo / Bard	Caves	River Running	Front Gate	Mountain Hall / Thorin	Arkenstone	Cave Door	Through Dragon's Lair
V	15-19	Thorin / Goblins	Eagles / Beorn	Dark Battlefield	Front Gate	Bridge at Edge of Wild	Home / Self	Treasure / Peace	Siege	•••••

Demo

savior does appear to work a *eucatastrophe* at the moment of direst peril. Bilbo participates in this pattern progressively: in the first part he is saved by luck and watches as Gandalf saves the others, in the second he saves himself but cannot save others, in the third he saves himself and others, in the fourth he contributes a collective effort of salvation, and in the fifth (a strange culmination suggesting a complex moral or theological position) he makes great sacrifice and is honored for it, but is unable to affect the outcome. Salvation comes, so to speak, from unearned grace, from the sudden arrival of forces beyond human prediction or control.

In each part Bilbo is rewarded for service, for growing unselfishness, but perhaps more for a willingness to act decisively, to move outward from the passive stance in which Gandalf finds him in the beginning, smoking by the door of his well-stocked hole.

7

Into the Lone-Lands

A DOUBTFUL DEPARTURE

The first part of *The Hobbit,* narrating Bilbo's journey to the "Edge of the Wild," is the briefest of the five parts and sets the pattern for the others. It begins with Bilbo still in the role of fussy homebody, more housekeeper than hero, meeting the wandering wizard with a double reaction—avoidance and fascination. He greets Gandalf with an empty, habitual "good morning," a social formality, and tries to dismiss the wizard with the same false phrase. This suggests in Bilbo a type of arrested development that Erich Neumann, in his psychological study of the symbolism of dragon tales, describes as "captivity." Here the hero's ego "remains totally dependent upon the father as the representative of collective norms. . . . and, as though castrated by convention, loses the higher half of its dual nature."[1] Bilbo is bound to the house of his father, of whom he is a "second edition" (12). Against this background, Gandalf is a spiritual "father" sent to wake the hobbit out of his dreamlike "castration"—and an analogue of Father Francis Morgan, Tolkien's guardian during his adolescent years.

Bilbo's nearly lost higher half is ready to respond. His slip of the tongue (almost calling the old Tookish days "interesting" and then recanting) shows that he is fascinated with the disruptive promise of the wizard, the memories of fireworks and journeys into the unknown. When Gandalf offers to send Bilbo on an adventure, the hobbit ducks behind social formality with the foolish answer, "Sorry! I don't want any adventures, thank you." But then his own doubleness betrays him into growth. What may seem a last formality is, in fact, an acceptance of adventure, as he reflexively invites the wizard to tea and even mentions "tomorrow" (15). Immediately, the hobbit wonders "what on earth" he said that for; but the most amateur analyst has no trouble explaining it. The buried personality within Bilbo Baggins has broken free and spoken. The Took made him do it.

Tolkien, though suspicious of psychological interpretations (*Letters,* 288), was nevertheless an astute practical psychologist. By the next day Bilbo is in Baggins mode once again and has "almost forgotten" about the invitation; he has repressed the disruptive scene of the day before, especially those parts in which his buried side spoke. Suspecting this, the wizard has arranged to gradually seduce Bilbo into Tookishness. Tolkien slips into nursery-tale cuteness during the long "Unexpected Party" scene, with dwarves imposing on the fussy hobbit and threatening to break dishes as they wash up. This part reads at best like an expanded Grimm tale, at worst like Walt Disney, whose popular *Snow White* Tolkien detested (*Letters,* 17). He admitted that his book "can be seen to begin in what might be called a more 'whimsy' mode, and in places even more facetious, and move steadily to a more serious or significant, and more consistent and historical" (*Letters,* 298).

The effect is artistically defensible. The early whimsy counterbalances the later epic style in a meaningful way: the foolish party scene suggests the foolishness of the Baggins personality, while the later style shows the emergence of the Took. But, of course, first-time readers cannot know this; so the slapstick humor and facetious style (along with a flood of unfamiliar Norse names) have put off thousands of readers who might have enjoyed the rest of the book. Tolkien repented this "silliness of manner," which he had mistakenly felt obliged to include in a "children's story" (*Letters,* 215), and made deep revisions in the first chapter. If the 1966 revision is still afflicted with "writing down" for children, the 1938 edition was much worse.

The tone grows more serious late in the first chapter, when darkness falls and the dwarves describe in song their hope to regain the Mountain where their ancestors were once rich and powerful—to reclaim ancestral treasure from a dragon who has blighted everything for miles around. Here is some of the best balladry in all of Tolkien's verse-laced fiction—for instance, when the approaching dragon is described through his effects: wind and fire in the trees before he bodily appears. The effect is at once cinematic and reminiscent of *Beowulf* and other medieval poetry (22). If you want mainstream poetry, look elsewhere, but here is mastery of a traditional craft.

The song awakens "something Tookish," a wish to wear a sword and see mountains, but the feeling fades when Thorin, leader of the dwarves, speaks in grim prose about suicidal risks. The hobbit faints and is put to bed like a child. Soon after, however, he is inflamed again with Tookish courage when he overhears a dwarf insulting him. Though physically weak, Bilbo has the steely "honor" of a Beowulf. He counters the dwarf's insult with a hyperbolic boast that traps him into accompanying the dwarves who, though experienced travelers, have no real plan for regaining their treasure (22). The force that drives them is indeed suicidal, a compound of anger and baseless faith. Absurdly, they expect the hobbit, whom Gandalf has designated a "burglar," to devise a plan. Their only hope is a treasure map (that staple of boy's fiction) rescued from Thorin's deranged and dying father, a map showing a secret entrance into the Mountain.

The hobbit's fear and the dwarves' rash faith (what the Greeks called *hubris*) are common variants in the mythological dragon fights described by Neumann. The dwarves, though bearded, act with a rashness characteristic of adolescent heroes who become tragic victims, such as Oedipus and Adonis; and, indeed, the leader of the dwarves will become such a victim. "To fly too high and fall, to go too deep and get stuck, these are alike symptoms of an overvaluation of the ego that ends in disaster, death, or madness" (Neumann 1954, 188). The dwarves are inflated by irrational impulses—complexes from the unconscious—and are easy victims of the devouring powers they go to face. Redeeming heroism is conquest of fear, not denial of it, and Bilbo is an important counterbalance to the dwarves precisely because he feels fear, is conscious of his vulnerability, and yet has the courage to move from his womblike home into danger. Without his timid powers, as we see repeatedly in the story, the hubris of the dwarves—their blind stubbornness and greed—leads them into traps. They demonstrate that impulse, however "brave," is no substitute for insight. Bravery built on macho denial is deadly.

In the second chapter we have another page or two, happily the last, of Baggins as *Hausfrau* (a role perhaps dwelt on too long to hold the interest of young readers). He has again slipped into semiconscious passivity. He has overslept and, as if the night before were a dream, is enjoying a second breakfast when Gandalf hustles him off naked—that is, without hat, cloak, or pocket-handkerchiefs—on the road to the lawless east. The symbolism here is of birth, or rather of rebirth, the first of several rebirths in the story.

An Apprentice Hero

After weeks of travel, Bilbo and the dwarves are running out of food as they cross a swollen river on a black, soggy night. Bilbo is more Baggins than Took: he wishes he was at home by his warm fire (35). As if in perverse answer to his wish, the dwarves see glints of a fire in a grove near the road, a fire that the expedition burglar is obliged to investigate. Of course Bilbo is reluctant, but Tookish honor compels him, as well as a touch of honest pride. He knows that hobbits walk more quietly than dwarves.

What Bilbo finds are giant trolls hungry for human flesh. Critics who have applied Jungian psychological terms to the story have identified a later character, Gollum, as Bilbo's "shadow," the figure representing the dark side of his personality. But the trolls represent a more primitive and collective shadow, three giant incarnations of infantile hunger. Though they share a fire, William, Bert, and Tom are creatures of selfish appetite, quarreling like greedy children. It is like when Alice, shrunken to a height of just a few inches, is almost trampled by a playful puppy the size of a cart horse.[2] A small vice, like a small puppy, may seem harmless, but a change in scale shows its destructiveness. When Bilbo sat down to a solitary second breakfast, ignoring the quest he had agreed to, he displayed a selfish fixation on food that the trolls display on a monstrous scale. Such an infantile fixation, though small compared to the trolls', may be deadly in the quest for individuation. This is something that Bilbo must overcome if he is to become a hero.

Given Tolkien's professional specialization in Old Norse and northern English literature, giant trolls are obvious folks to encounter on a perilous road east. Snorri Sturluson's Old Norse *Edda* tells of two occasions when Thor is away from Asgard because he has gone to the east to fight trolls; and in an older poem, Loki teases Thor about his encounter with a giant "on the East-road." At the end of the world, the giants will attack from the east.[3] Lost on a road east, the dwarves could have used the advice that Brynhild gives Sigurd in *The Saga of the Volsungs*, a Norse classic young Tolkien read and retold to his school friends (Carpenter, 46): "If you travel a road where evil creatures dwell, be wary. Although caught by nightfall, do not take shelter near the road, for foul beings who bewilder men often live there."[4] Also, there are many medieval Irish analogues to Bilbo's situation, including an episode when Finn, traveling at night, investigates a fire in a deserted valley and meets a household of giants, the lady of the house having three heads. A fight breaks out around Finn, and he is saved by the rising sun, which makes the giants disappear.[5] The analogues here are obvious, though the material is shifted and recolored. Tolkien created freely and flexibly from the raw material of myth and legend.

The fact that the trolls are three suggests that the problem they represent is collective, indeed not Bilbo's *individual* shadow, but general weakness that must be overcome before individual development can begin. Also, threeness is the number of the Fates and of similar goddesses in many cultures who predict or govern the future,[6] and it is the first symbolic number, the number of movement forward, the number associated with "demons of time."[7] Here, in almost trivial events within a scene as comic as it is frightening, the future is cast. Bilbo's often-mentioned "luck" originates in his failed private effort to master the trolls. A clear chain of events will lead from his "accidental" finding of a key to the troll's cave on to the future death of the dragon. He will use the key to get a weapon, the weapon to keep the ring, the ring and sword to save his companions, and so forth. Here again is the pattern of incremental repetition, the spiral.

Commissioned to act by the dwarves, Bilbo is forced to improvise from old stories. He debuts as fairy-tale hero by modeling his behavior on fairy tales. The stories that Bilbo recalls are, of course, Tolkien's improvisations but resemble European folktales of quick little heroes overcoming stupid giants, such as "Jack and the Beanstalk" and "The Brave Little Tailor" and particularly one tale from the Grimm collection, "The Expert Huntsman." A small fellow lost in the woods creeps up to a fire and finds three giants roasting an ox. From the shadows the lad shoots meat from their hands, then wins their confidence and beheads them.[8] Bilbo, recalling similar tales, selects a simple trick, picking a pocket.

But William's magic purse sounds an alarm, and the troll grabs Bilbo. Judging the hobbit too small to cook, the trolls ask if he is alone, and like a good story-book Jack, Bilbo lies. He is not yet skilled at deceptive speech, but his confused, pitiful words have an ironic good effect. They provoke a fight among the trolls, and Bilbo crawls to safety. The whole horrific scene is antiheroic, with Cockney accents, punning words, slapstick fights. The three trolls become The Three Stooges. This may go with the territory: Homer used similar grim humor in his account of Odysseus and the Cyclops. Still, it is easy to miss, under the burlesque tone, some striking parallels between Bilbo's encounter with the trolls and his much later encounter with the dragon, parallels that show how much he has grown through the months, miles, and chapters. When Bilbo later sneaks into Smaug's lair, he is able to burgle a two-handled cup without the dragon's noticing and return to chat in polished deceptive tones reminiscent of Old Norse word combats, managing neither to lie nor to reveal very much.

By the end of the book, he is a competent Jack, but in the troll episode he is still incompetent, saved only by Pigletlike insignificance.

Meanwhile, Bilbo has failed to warn the dwarves, and as they rashly approach the fire, the trolls catch them one by one in smelly bags. Thorin, like Odysseus following his men to Circe's house, is forewarned and puts up a fight, but he is strangely not armed. Soon all the dwarves are "nearly suffocated" as the trolls discuss plans to cook them (42). The bagging of the dwarves, while Bilbo remains free to breathe, is twice repeated in *The Hobbit,* when spiders bag them in silk in Mirkwood and when they are shut in barrels to escape elves. Throughout the book danger is claustrophobic: seen sometimes as fire and wounding, but usually as suffocating enclosure, like Jonah in the belly of a great fish or Fortunato walled up in a cellar in Poe's "The Cask of Amontillado." Though the dwarves are twice scheduled to be eaten, the actual cooking and chewing are twice delayed while they helplessly await rescue.

THE WORLD AS MOTHER: MATURATION AS BIRTH

A constant throughout the story is Bilbo's skill at avoiding entrapment. He may be too small to threaten his foes directly, but luck and courage make him an escape artist, a lightweight wrestler who seldom pins others but cannot himself be pinned. Baggins of Bag-End has lived his life in a cul-de-sac, and once out, he is hard to bag. As mythological symbols, *bagging* and *escaping bagging* are strongly connected to the theme of Bilbo's maturation. *The Great Mother,* Erich Neumann's monumental Jungian study of female symbols in art and psychology, describes the elementary character of the Terrible Mother as "*holding fast, fixating,* and *ensnaring,* which indicates the dangerous and deadly aspects of the Great Mother, just as the opposite pole shows her aspect of life and growth" (Neumann 1963, 65). Though the symbolic mother may be positive and transforming, leading to fuller life, she becomes positive only after she releases her offspring, male or female. Then she appears as a vessel of protection and rebirth, not a suffocating bag.

This mother is often shrouded in symbols and does not appear as a woman at all but as a cave in the earth or as a devouring monster. Neumann analyzes a wide range of symbols that have been used to trace the emergence of human consciousness from infantile unconsciousness through the hero's victory over the negative mother, often seen as a dragon. This heroic process, Neumann argues, is part of the history of humanity, but also a process that each of us must undergo to mature as individuals. Killing or escaping the negative mother to be born into the arms of the positive one, the sunlit Mother Earth, is symbolically the process of growing up, and everyone who grows up is symbolically a dragon slayer.[9]

Bilbo is such a hero. His mother is dead—that is, buried in his unconsciousness and denied, threatening him as a negative force. Such a buried psychological force manifests itself in real life as what psychologists call *projections,* patterns of our minds that we see as if cast by a movie projector onto the outside world—and in fiction such a buried force is represented by the symbolic contents of the story. Out there, everywhere he turns, Bilbo meets (as we may through projection) symbols of the vengeful mother, images of repressed Tookishness, terrors that become positive as he masters them and is reborn.

Neumann's focus on the symbolic mother in developmental psychology is authorized by the early references to Belladonna Took, Bilbo's mother, as well as by Tolkien's structuring the hero's evolution in terms of his struggle with a buried Took side. And we should remember that the darker aspects of Neumann's symbolic mother are often disguised in inanimate or even masculine images, but are defined by their devouring nature and the promise of rebirth when they are overcome. Though the trolls have masculine names, they combine the hungry selfish child and the Terrible Mother—huge as a mother is to a baby and threatening to devour, to trap in bags, like the giant spiders who are more transparently female in Tolkien's mythology. Bilbo's escape from the trolls also launches his heroism: crawling away (the infant's first gesture of independence), Bilbo discovers a key to the trolls' cave, from which he gains a sword, symbol of the phallic power of the hero to escape entrapment.

Though there is no sex in this book (and no female but a buried mother), Bilbo twice performs the symbolic equivalent of the sexual mastery of Odysseus over Circe, the transforming negative mother (Neumann 1963, 83), which occurs when the Greek hero shows her his sword and she takes him into her bed. Bilbo's emulation of Odysseus, like so much else in *The Hobbit,* is progressive: in the encounter with Gollum, Bilbo only shows the sword (68), but later he thrusts it into a hungry spider's eyes (135).

SWORDS AND SOURCES

In the troll episode Bilbo is still impotent, however, and the dwarves are freed from their bags by the transforming skills of Gandalf. Like a stage ventriloquist, Gandalf secretly imitates the trolls and keeps them quarreling until the sunrise turns them to stone. In Norse mythology, dwarves, like vampires, must be underground by sunrise, or they turn back into "the stuff of the mountains they are made of" (42). The sun is called *Dvalins leika,* "deceiver of Dwalin," for this reason (Bellows, 188), and Thor practices a trick very like Gandalf's on Alvis, a dwarf who has come to ask for his daughter's hand in marriage. The encounter ends with Thor's speech: "The sun has caught thee dwarf! / Now the sun shines here in the hall" (Bellows, 194). In another Old Norse poem, two heroes defeat a giant troll by keeping her talking until the sun rises. The results are the same: "as a harbor mark shall men mock at thee, / Where in stone thou shalt ever stand" (Bellows, 284). These formulas compare with Gandalf's, "Dawn take you all, and be stone to you" (42).

A footnote in R. W. Chambers's classic study of *Beowulf* states, in relation to a giantess that a hero has fought all night, "A night-troll, if caught by the sunrise, was supposed to turn to stone."[10] The petrification of trolls is such a commonplace in medieval Norse and English, Tolkien's fields, that he is obviously sharing his own perspective when he suggests offhand that we already know about it (42). This trait of trolls, presumably as familiar to Tolkien as clocks and beer, is casually drawn into his fictive world, where his offhand remark takes the marvel for granted and encourages readers to do the same.

Fortunately, before dawn petrifies the trolls, the key falls out of William's pocket—falls when they are fighting each other as a result of Bilbo's words—and the hobbit sees it. It is the key to a cave of swords and bones. The symbolic link between key and sword is obvious: both act by penetrating and are symbols of the hero's power to open what is closed. The travelers have inexplicably neglected to arm themselves at this point (though the dwarves are metal workers and travel with musical instruments), and the symbolism is clear when they trade Bilbo's key for marvelous swords from the trolls' grisly cave. The fact that Thorin and Company have not earlier armed themselves makes little realistic sense; there is no mention even of the mattocks that Thorin's kinsmen use as weapons later in the story (235). It does make sense as part of the symbolic grammar of Bilbo's maturation. The hobbit is the focal point of the symbolic structure, so logically the party remains unarmed until he has (to borrow a phallic cliché) "earned his spurs." Like Sir Percival and other Arthurian novices, Bilbo takes arms from his first (however ironic) military conquest. Finding a bright blade in the troll hoard, he realizes his boyish wish to "wear a sword instead of a walking-stick" (22), though it becomes his custom to wear his blade modestly "inside his breeches" (66). Of course, this blade will save him when he faces a devouring monster in a dark hole.

Thorin and Gandalf find blades, too, marvelous swords suggesting Arthur's Excalibur, Roland's Durendal, Sigurd's Gram, and Beowulf's "old giant-made" sword. Both the lore of old marvelous swords and their acquisition from the lairs of night monsters are commonplace in medieval stories. Beowulf, of course, finds the marvelous sword (apparently the only one that can cut the troll he is fighting) among the looted war gear in her own lair (line 1557). In the Old Norse saga that most suggests *Beowulf,* the same one in which a troll is turned to stone, Grettir sees a sword hanging in a troll cave, along with treasure and the remains of victims (Chambers, 180); in another part of the story he wins an old sword and treasure in an underground fight with an undead corpse.[11] Similarly, in a saga edited by Tolkien's son, a marvelous sword is given to the hero's mother by the awakened corpse of her father,[12] and an undead corpse gives the hero a sword in the *Sturlunga Saga*[13]—much as Odin, lord of the slain, gives Gram to his hero-victim Sigmund (*Volsungs,* 38).

Night walkers and demonic cannibals, devourers of the living, are associated throughout mythology with the unquiet dead, and the bones in the cave symbolize this and echo the frequent arming of heroes by the dead or by gods of the dead. Tolkien draws, again quite casually, a wealth of arcane lore into the lucid narrative of *The Hobbit.* The symbolic power of the sword is ancient: perhaps there is no clearer image of the sword's relationship to the underworld than Odysseus holding back the literally blood-thirsty dead in Hades with his bronze sword, the same tool that earlier mastered Circe.

In the developmental psychology of the dragon-slaying myth, swords represent the power of the hero to defend against the devouring forces of the unconscious, the dark world beneath and beyond ordinary will; and often these dark forces, as part of the healthy psyche's tendency to grow toward wholeness, provide the hero-ego with the tool for their own subjugation. The blades that defeat later night-walkers naturally come from a cave of night-walkers, though the transcendent goodness of the blades is clear. Elves forged them to fight goblins.

In the Nurturing Valley

After supplying themselves from the cave, the dwarves journey through a symbol-soaked landscape to the Last Homely House, where elves welcome them. The eerie landscape the party crosses after escaping the trolls is a virtual allegory of perilous Mother Earth, she who nurtures and devours. Mountains loom in the background, near but far, and in the foreground is a plain interrupted by narrow clefts full of water and vegetation. The only safe path is marked by a trail of white stones, reminiscent of "Hansel and Gretel" (that tale of a murderous mother and a cannibal witch), and travelers not guided by these stones would find their way blocked by "dark ravines" or deadly bogs that look like "green pleasant places" (47). Geologically, this all seems unlikely, so many valleys, so deep, and bogs on the plateau not draining into them, but the improbability merely suggests a landscape on the edge of allegory, effective not only as sensuous description, but also as a fabric of symbols.

The hungry journey over a perilous plain toward visible but distant mountains, like so much in *The Hobbit,* echoes a situation in *King Solomon's Mines*—in this case the trek across the African desert toward mountains. Rider Haggard, however, makes the analogue between Mother Earth and the female body explicit by naming the mist-gauzed mountains that are the thirsty all-male party's destination "Sheba's Breasts."[14] What is cloaked in symbol by Tolkien is utterly explicit in Haggard's description. While Tolkien simply writes of his mountains that "the tips of snow-peaks gleamed" (46), Haggard is anatomically specific: "on the top of each was a vast round hillock covered with snow, exactly corresponding to the nipples on the female breast" (85).

Like Haggard's Allan Quartermain, Bilbo survives only because his party has foreknowledge of the right trail and a guru to guide them to the nurturing aperture (a water hole in Haggard, and secret valley in Tolkien) on the plain swelling below the mountains. Of course, Tolkien's passage, unlike Haggard's, works as real symbolism—that is without readers' necessarily noticing it—and it need not be made explicit to produce the appropriate effect on readers. Nevertheless, the absence of living female characters does raise the question, Where is woman? And the ride toward the Last Homely House, glossed by *King Solomon's Mines* and symbolic studies such as Neumann's, suggests one obvious answer: She is under Bilbo's feet. It is she to whom the old man in Chaucer's *Pardoner's Tale* speaks when he strikes the earth "which is my mother's gate" with his staff and cries, "Mother, let me in!"[15]

Suddenly, with night coming on and food bags empty, Gandalf's horse slips on a sudden downhill slope. This is no grave, but a nurturing refuge, the green and secret valley of Rivendell, where Elrond presides over an enclave of elves hidden in twilight and song. Of all of Tolkien's humanlike races, the elves are closest to the earth, and not just the earth of "masculine" daylight, but the sinister earth of "feminine" night. They defend themselves with natural magic and sing under the stars. If the heroes in Tolkien's story are masculine, the earth feminine, then the elves as a race are androgynous mediators, good friends of twilight earth. And Elrond is even more clearly between worlds because he is half elf, half human.

With the mention of Elrond, Bilbo's story is linked to *The Silmarillion,* a mythological cycle that Tolkien had been writing since World War I, elaborating the vast migrations of the elves. This cycle, written in a style reminiscent of Old Testament histories, was repeatedly revised and finally published in 1977. *The Hobbit* and *The Silmarillion* were originally not connected. Bilbo's adventures began as a bedtime story unrelated to the myths; indeed, Tolkien claimed to have used the name Elrond only because he found it hard to invent good new names (*Letters,* 347). In any case, Elrond (who appears in mythological manuscripts as early as 1926) has the elvish trait of immortality. When he mentions the fall of Gondolin, he refers to his family history, almost his memory. He is more than six thousand years old, and his father Eärendil (the planet Venus) was one of the few survivors of that famous elvish stronghold, the sacking of which Tolkien described in an early tale, *The Fall of Gondolin.*[16] Later, after fighting heroically against the satanic archenemy of the good, Elrond chose not to emigrate beyond the earth to Elvenhome and, held back by his human half, "ruled in the West of the world."[17] With mention of Elrond and Gondolin, and fabled swords from past millennia, Tolkien discovers a subtext that will lend his whimsical tale the resonances to make it a classic. Just after the publication of *The Hobbit* he wrote, "My tale is not consciously based on any other book—save one," his own unpublished Elvish history (*Letters,* 31).

Elrond's Edenic little valley, which functions in Tolkien's story much the way Mackenzie's mission station does in Haggard's *King Solomon's Mines,* is called the Last Homely House. It closes the first part of the story, the first "fairy-story," by offering Bilbo and his friends rest and supplies for the next leg of their trek. In fact, though it is the last hospitable dwelling west of the Misty Mountains, it is only the first of a series of places of rest and resupply, "Homely Houses" that give closure to parts of *The Hobbit.*

In keeping with the timelessness of the elves on the twilight edge of human consciousness,[18] the days at Elrond's house pass like a dream. Elves are the good people of borderline and dreams. According to the Elvish history written when *The Hobbit* was begun, they were born under a sky of stars before the creation of the sun. Little happens among them that Bilbo can retell, though there are many songs and stories, much late sleeping and comfort: "days that are good to spend are soon told about, and not much to listen to" (50). The days at Rivendell, like a warm bath of healing, suggest Circe's hospitality after Odysseus has mastered her negative transformations. The psychological process is this: if we can only defeat night trolls, the elves will take us in and show us the stars.

Then, on the final day of the visit, in a scene that recalls one from *Beowulf,* Elrond reads the swords from the troll lair. The half-elven king can read ancient runes and learns the names and origins of the swords from inscriptions on them: "These are old swords, very old swords of the High Elves of the West, my kin. They were made in Gondolin for the Goblin-wars." Elrond reads the name on each sword and traces them to a war (51) shortly before a continental sinking that in Tolkien's myths corresponds to the Great Flood. Tolkien acknowledged the influence of *Beowulf* (*Letters,* 31), and the parallels here are striking. Shortly before saying goodbye to Beowulf, the old king of the Danes reads runes on the hilt of the ancient sword, "work of giants," which the hero hands to him: "he scrutinized the hilt, the ancient heirloom, upon which was inscribed the rise of the primeval strife when the flood, the rushing deep, destroyed the brood of giants." In "runic letters" on the hilt Hrothgar reads the name of the sword's first owner.[19] Coincidental with introduction of Elrond to *The Hobbit* is the introduction of a strong echo of *Beowulf.* An epic tone is established and whimsy exorcised.

ORIGINS AND BEGINNINGS

Thus, after a shaky start, an almost-false beginning barely covered over with post-1937 revisions, Tolkien finds at Elrond's house the deep roots of a heroic fiction for his century. It is here that the tone solidifies, taking on muted resonances of *Beowulf,* Norse sagas, and the Bible, and the hobbit tale borrows high seriousness from a millennial history of struggles between good and evil, the Goblin-wars and the fall of Gondolin. Most of the revisions beyond this point were made not for style but for content, to bring the story in line with the revised history of Middle-earth that emerged as Tolkien wrote *The Lord of the Rings* and Bilbo's magic ring became the One Ring of Power. Though the 1937 text does not harmonize with Tolkien's later gospel, after Rivendell it is stylistically sound and heroic in tone. The "children's-book" fatuities of the early chapters vanish like mist, leaving only a few odd wisps behind.

In his book *Beginnings,* Edward Said distinguishes between "beginnings" and "origins" after asking, "Is the beginning of a given work its real beginning, or is there some other, secret point that more authentically starts the work off?"[20] The historical point of beginning of *The Hobbit* is well documented. Tolkien wrote the first sentence spontaneously on an examination booklet (*Letters,* 215), so it was (in Jungian terms) an eruption of the unconscious in a moment of dulled attention—or *abaissement du niveau mental.* He literally did not know what he had begun. Later he developed the story as family entertainment, without literary intentions, seeing it as a sort of elaborate game like the Father Christmas letters he wrote to his children. He did not design it initially to connect with the Elvish histories he had already written nor intentionally model it on *Beowulf,* which he was studying at the time. This may be important. The works he had written with serious literary intent had not found publishers. They are written in a dense, archaic style that suggests scripture or ancient epics in translation and would not have sold well to a reading public unacquainted with his fantasy world. Probably the very lack of seriousness surrounding *The Hobbit* led him to use a lighter touch, a style in which he could sell his mythology to a reading public. The false beginning that leaves its traces in the first chapters of *The Hobbit* may have been an essential ritual in the writing process, a gesture of literary relaxation.

While the *beginning* of any work consists of its first pages and their composition, this beginning may be only a search for the

61

preconditions that allow the book to be successfully completed. Such preconditions are the book's *origins,* the things that must "preexist" it, or perhaps the *point of origin* may be the point where these preconditions come to light. The *beginning* is the planting of the seed; the *origins* are the DNA of the seed, the chemistry of the soil, and whatever else preexists the growth process and yet only becomes manifest through it. The origins of Tolkien's completed story include his philological scholarship, years of writing Elvish history and language, intuitive grasp of the methods of myth and fairy story, and Thomist reflections on good and evil. With the first line, indeed the first chapters of *The Hobbit,* he has only begun; he has not yet tunnelled down to these origins, the strengths that make the book and its sequels great. But at Rivendell he makes contact; all of the story before Elrond may be seen as prologue, necessary beginning, and Elrond the point of origin. Here an egg hatched by a duck manifests its origins in the profile of a swan.

At Rivendell, too, Tolkien completes the pattern that he sketches in his lecture "On Fairy-Stories"—what will be the structural unit throughout *The Hobbit.* In the second and third chapters, after the expository first chapter, Bilbo and his companions run short of food and encounter a body of water just before meeting deadly, devouring foes in a dark, enclosed place. Then Bilbo's heroism is tested and he or the dwarves are either buried alive or trapped in containers (in this part, bags). When conditions seem hopeless, an unexpected rescue produces a sudden joyous turn. Bilbo receives a reward as a result of his heroic test. Then the party crosses another body of water to a "Homely House," where a host resupplies and advises them. There will be variations in this pattern, dislocations and doublings; but the fairy-story form, echoing universal myths of maturation and the solar hero, is completed at Elrond's house and will be repeated four more times.

8

Bilbo's Adventures in Wilderland

A Larger Landscape

After the confined early chapters, taking place mostly indoors or in a circle of firelight, part 2 opens out to spectacular scenery and violent action. Bilbo crosses mountains and plains, explores caves and flies with eagles. He is taken prisoner, defends himself with a sword, and is almost burned alive and eaten by wolves. The episodes between Elrond's house and Mirkwood, with patches of strong fantasy description, display strengths that made Tolkien a master of heroic fantasy.

After days on crooked, cold mountain paths, Bilbo is again thinking of "safe and comfortable things" (54) when a frightful thunderstorm forces the company to shelter in a little cave that, unknown to them, adjoins a network of goblin-infested tunnels. Bilbo saves the dwarves this time, though in conjunction with Gandalf, when he awakens just in time to call a warning and prevent the wizard from being captured by goblins. But everyone else is captured and bound in chains, including Baggins and the baggage—the all-important food. Using one of the swords from the lair that Bilbo's key opened, Gandalf rescues the dwarves, and they flee down black tunnels, where a goblin ambush leaves Bilbo stunned and abandoned in the dark.

Waking, he crawls through the gloom until he touches a cold metal ring and puts it into his pocket. This is, says Tolkien, "a turning point in his career" (65). His Baggins personality dominant, he sits down to think about bacon and eggs and is about to foolishly light his pipe when he discovers the elvish knife hidden under his clothes. The blade awakens something Tookish in him, and the hobbit becomes a reluctant warrior and explorer, a sword-boy trotting along with one hand gripping his weapon, the other feeling his way along the dark wall.

The tunnel dead-ends at a subterranean lake where Gollum, the fallen hobbit who will play a pivotal role in *The Lord of the Rings*, paddles about in the dark and eats whatever happens by. Like the goblins, he is a cannibal, for he eats goblins and wants to eat Bilbo. Because of Bilbo's bright sword, however, Gollum proposes a riddle contest. Bilbo, like Oedipus, must answer or die. When he luckily wins with the last question (not a riddle), "What have I got in my pocket?" (73), Gollum searches for his ring of invisibility and, failing to find it, guesses that it is in Bilbo's pocket. Gollum's mumbles reveal to Bilbo the powers of the ring he has found. The 1937 edition differs from the post–*Lord-of-the-Rings* edition at this point, but in both Gollum leads Bilbo to the exit (where he mercifully leaps over the little monster to avoid killing him after 1951). Bilbo invisibly dodges goblin guards and escapes into sunlight. He has passed through the mountains to reach the eastern slopes.

Bilbo has Tookishly determined to return for his comrades when suddenly he hears dwarf voices and discovers Gandalf and the dwarves safe nearby. Hurrying downhill to avoid goblin pursuit, the party is trapped in trees later that night by hundreds of strange wolves called Wargs. Gandalf scorches the Wargs with wizard fire, but the tables are turned when goblins appear and stoke fires around the trees. Suddenly, in a classic *eucatastrophe*, giant eagles—"not kindly birds" but noble enemies of goblins (93)—lift the company to the safety of their mountain ledges. The eagles feed the dwarves and set them down far from their pursuers and nearer their destination, on the plain beyond the mountains.

On the Carrock, a hill of rock in a river bend, the wizard says that he must leave the dwarves after he has seen them supplied at the house of Beorn, a burly vegetarian who can turn himself into a bear. Whereas Elrond was half elf, Beorn is (in effect) half bear. Just as the dwarves took refuge from trolls with elves, they take refuge from wolves with a bear, and it is consistent that birds carry them. The dwarves arrive a few at a time at Beorn's house as Gandalf tells of their adventures—a variation on the gradual approach that worked well at Bilbo's house and disastrously with the trolls. After a supper like none they had eaten "since they left the Last Homely House" (111), they sing and sleep, hearing the tramping of many bears in the courtyard outside. Beorn directs the dwarves to the Elf-path through the dark forest Mirkwood. They say goodbye to Gandalf at the edge.

The same basic structural elements are here, but doubled or tripled. There are three sets of foes—goblins, Gollum, and Wargs—and three distinct *eucatastrophes*. Again danger falls in conditions of darkness and hunger, at night or in caverns. As in part 1, the company is first saved by Gandalf, though Bilbo helps this time. Bilbo rescues himself, but no one else, from the second peril, and the third rescue is by the eagles, symbols of divine intervention when even Gandalf's powers are inadequate. The test Bilbo faces in part 2 involves simply his resolution to act alone in the dark, to use his sword and wits like a hero. Passing this test leaves him with a prize, a ring of invisibility, which allows him to become a genuine hero able to save the comrades and destroy a dragon. There is water again at crucial points of the story—the lake just before Bilbo meets Gollum and the Great River at the Carrock just before Beorn's hall. Again Bilbo and the others are trapped and bound, if not bagged. And here, for the first time, we have a solar night-sea journey, a passage through darkness under the earth from west to east, symbol of the cosmic cycle of death and rebirth at a higher plane.

A STORM AND THE ABSENCE OF WOMEN

Part 2 begins with description that, while tinged with fantasy, is remarkably realistic. The author is recalling personal experience. In 1911 Tolkien hiked with a heavy pack through Switzerland, an episode he identified as the model for Bilbo's mountain crossing. A fierce thunderstorm in real life drove the party to shelter in a cattle shed, not a goblin cave, but boulders loosened by melting snow did roll among the travelers, barely missing Tolkien in one instance (*Letters*, 309). The slide down a rocky slope into pines west of the mountains (88) is also an incident from the Swiss trip, which involved cooking outdoors and sleeping "rough" (*Letters*, 392). Add goblins and Wargs to the Swiss trip, and you have a fair replica of Bilbo's mountain crossing.

One important difference, however, is that the older adult who conducted young Tolkien on the trip (the Gandalf-figure) was his botanist aunt (*Letters*, 308), and this suggests one obvious way of dealing with the absence of women in *The Hobbit*. Perhaps figures who would ordinarily have been women have been fictionally costumed and recast as men, without wholly losing their original character. The Swiss trek with his maiden aunt is a clear instance. The actual trip involved, in Tolkien's own words, "a mixed party about the same size as the company in *The Hobbit*" (*Letters*, 309). As the biographical event was transformed into fiction, the men and women became male dwarves. Tolkien's fiction may be said to dramatize the "common gender" value of the pronoun *he*, which until the 1970s was accepted as referring indifferently to either male or female persons. It is a man's world. One reason for this may be a desire to avoid sexual themes while dealing with close relationships. Tolkien felt that in the "fallen world" sex spoils relationships between men and women: friendship is almost impossible because sex is the devil's "favorite subject" (*Letters*, 48). So presumably Tolkien shifts sexual identities to invent a sexless world.

The submerged feminine is particularly implicit in Gandalf, who doubles as surrogate mother and father to Bilbo and performs the transforming function that Jung attributes to a man's inner feminine image, or "anima." Biographically speaking, we know that a mature priest assumed the role of Tolkien's mother after she died. Mythologically speaking, we find Erich Neumann emphasizing the gender ambiguity of wizard figures. After noting their originally feminine character, Neumann says, "Even in a later period the male shaman or seer is in high degree 'feminine,' since he is dependent on his anima aspect. And for this reason he often appears in woman's dress" (Neumann 1963, 296). Gandalf does indeed dress as only a woman (or priest) would in Tolkien's England, in pointed hat, long robe, and silver scarf (13). Even his phallic fire-tipped staff is in modern stories associated more with fairy godmothers than wizards, more with witches than warlocks.

Gandalf's role parallels Merlin's in the King Arthur stories, but also Glinda's in *The Wizard of Oz*, the great-grandmother's in *The Princess and Curdie*, and Athena's in *The Odyssey*; and, of course, when Athena calls Telemachus to adventure, she is disguised as a man. Doubled gender is strikingly suggested by an illustration from E. A. Wyke Smith's 1927 *The Marvelous Land of Snergs*, which Tolkien read repeatedly to his children and modeled *The Hobbit* directly after (*Letters*, 215). This drawing shows a bearded figure looking like Gandalf riding a pony, but the actual subject is a disguised witch, Mother Meldrum, riding off with two good children trapped in baskets.[1] Here is a negative image of Gandalf doing what negative creatures do repeatedly in *The Hobbit*. So is Gandalf a positive mother? Indeed, he seems to function as Bilbo's fairy godmother, wand and all, and his actual physical form, though nominally masculine, is no less maternal than other fairy-tale proxies for the dead mother, such as the hazel tree cast in that role in the Grimm "Cinderella."

The absent feminine in Tolkien may, in other words, be present not only in Mother Nature and those dark caves but in the long-robed wizard with his stage beard, the androgynously glamorous elf-lord who is "kind as summer" (51), or the bearlike beekeeper who "loves his animals as his children" (119). It is possible to make too much of this, for even as characters act out the absent feminine, they remain literally male. Nevertheless, beyond being called *he*, Bilbo is scarcely more masculine than Dorothy. Though marginal female figures do appear in *The Lord of the Rings*, Bilbo's starkly womanless adventures can be explained by an unconscious or half-conscious pattern of alternation, pronoun shifts, and minor costume changes to "masculate" characters whose roles might suit actresses better than actors. Female readers may identify with characters who transcend masculine pronouns and act out "feminine" traits.

Indeed, what is macho in *The Hobbit* is bad. Androgyny, a blend of masculine and feminine traits, is the hobbit-hero's character. Thorin, the conventionally masculine leader of the dwarves, given to formal speeches and territorial boasts, makes peace with Bilbo in a speech that affirms androgynous devotion to kitchen and parlor: "If more of us valued food and cheer and song above hoarded gold, it would be a merrier world" (243). The dying dwarf king repents his earlier macho posturing, his stiff-necked insistence on personal rights in defiance of the common good. Courage is essential, and Bilbo is not lacking it, but the androgynous hero's courage (like Dorothy's when she defends her dog from the Cowardly Lion, who has defeated her companions[2]) is a response to humane necessity, not an act of gratuitous masculine will. Bilbo cooperates and shares; he does not compete to establish personal dominance. His most powerful stance is invisibility, not the claiming of territory. Like Bilbo, Tolkien's true military heroes fight reluctantly and only to the extent needed to protect themselves and the good. Violence is justified by the ideal of peace.[3] Bilbo, with courage and wisdom "blended in measure" (243), is concerned at the end not with treasure but with "going home soon" (245).

TOLKIEN'S INFERNO

In part 2 we find the typical beginning. Hardship drives the company into danger; in this case a storm and falling rocks, a war between heaven and earth, drive them to a cave. Hardships, says Neumann, are often "stations on the road leading through danger to salvation, through the extinction of death to rebirth and new life" (Neumann 1963, 76). The cave in the mountain is at once the body of the Great

Mother and the gate to the underworld, through which the solar hero must pass to be reborn. The great danger, of course, is that once he has taken shelter, subterranean forces will hold him forever. The danger of caves, Tolkien says, is that "you don't know how far they go back, sometimes, or where a passage behind may lead to, or what is waiting for you inside" (57). What is waiting, symbolically speaking, is the opposite of what we have labored to create in the world of sunlight, the inverse of the values we have chosen to affirm in conscious life. Under the earth is the world of demons.

So naturally, what comes out of a "crack" in the cave after Bilbo's company lapses into unconsciousness is a nonhuman species very much like the devils in Dante's *Inferno* and other Christian stories, a species symbolizing human vice. In *The Hobbit* they are called goblins, and though their behavior is collective, they are bound together by hatred, fear, and hunger, not fellowship or sympathy. They talk to their prisoners only as a prelude to torture and cannibalism. Tolkien copied his particular breed of goblins, with few alterations, from those in George MacDonald's juvenile classic *The Princess and the Goblin*. Like MacDonald's, Tolkien's goblins are unredeemably evil but are still a mortal flesh-and-blood species, like plague rats in the cellars of the mountains.

Like MacDonald, he describes a mountain honeycombed with tunnels, some mined, some natural, and inhabitants who are grotesque and cunning and roam at night. MacDonald's goblins, like Tolkien's, speak the language of men, have their own king, and aspire to conquer the surface world. Sounds of goblin feet pursue Bilbo's party underground (63), and MacDonald's Curdie hears "the sound of many soft feet" while hiding from goblins.[4] MacDonald's goblins, like Tolkien's, have a great torch-lit throne-room not far inside the mountain, and both have kings who express an inverted moral logic—describing events in a topsy-turvy way that identifies the interests of the unruly, night-loving goblins with good and anything to the contrary with evil. For them a "sun-person" is "fresh meat" (MacDonald, 101). In the brief speech in which the Great Goblin calls Thorin's people spies, thieves, murderers, and (worst of all) "friends of Elves" (61), Tolkien tries out a gesture that MacDonald uses repeatedly in *The Princess and the Goblin.* There is even a river in the heart of MacDonald's mountain, and MacDonald's boy hero is trapped in the mountain after he, like Bilbo, is hit in the head during a goblin attack and loses consciousness. Much like Bilbo, Curdie is alone and helpless under the mountain, with improvised rhymes "his only weapons" (MacDonald, 104). These similarities, however, are only symptomatic; reading either book after the other produces déjà vu. Tolkien's goblins, as he admitted, are MacDonald's rewritten (*Letters*, 178).

It is easy, with the right reading list, to locate stories that resemble *The Hobbit*, stories that are part of the tradition out of which it grew and are perhaps even direct "sources," such as *Beowulf*, the Eddas, and MacDonald. If we stop with simply demonstrating that sources are indeed sources, however, we gain little. For interpretive understanding we must take a step farther and ask how a work is different from its sources: what parts of MacDonald's goblin myth Tolkien rejected. Because the line of least resistance is to continue imitating, deviations from MacDonald's goblin myth should be read as strong gestures.

Tolkien's goblins are more grim and sinister than MacDonald's, who are played for comedy and are easily overcome (until he slips up) by a miner's boy singing verses (they hate music). MacDonald's goblins are complex, but their complexity is whimsical or satiric, suitable to the facetious tone that Tolkien indulged early in *The Hobbit* but abandoned at Elrond's house. MacDonald's tone is more like T. H. White's whimsical Arthurian court in *The Sword in the Stone* than Tolkien's increasingly serious Middle-earth. MacDonald's goblins are distinguished from "sun-people" by the fact that they have delicate ducklike feet with no separate toes and wear no shoes (except their queen, feared for her iron shoes). MacDonald's hero, Curdie, repels a crowd of goblins by stamping about, a scene that serves the purposes of MacDonald's story and may have allegorical purpose but is burlesque in mood, like the scuffling trolls early in *The Hobbit*.

Tolkien's goblins are grimly evil beings with none of the special sensitivities of MacDonald's, except sensitivity to sunlight, a trait of most evil things in Tolkien. So while MacDonald's goblins are so sensitive to rhyme that Curdie uses doggerel as an area weapon to clear tunnels, Tolkien's goblins sing their own cruel songs as they drag off victims. A dysfunctional goblin royal family is given pages of comic dialogue by MacDonald as Curdie eavesdrops, much like the comic troll dialogue in Tolkien's troll chapter. But Tolkien has turned a stylistic corner since then. His goblins are hysterical and collective but quite dangerous, capable of suicide attacks. They must be killed in the plain heroic way, with bloody swords. Goblins are demonic foes who, for all their lack of individual character, must be taken seriously.

While pruning down MacDonald's goblins, Tolkien does pause for almost half a page to describe goblin character in a way different from MacDonald. Cruel and disorderly, unable to make or enjoy beautiful things, Tolkien's are nevertheless gifted in the design and use of tools of destruction. They are blamed for the destructive inventions of the machine age, especially weapons of mass destruction, "for wheels and engines and explosions always delighted them" (60). Here Tolkien is projecting on MacDonald's goblins his own vision of twentieth-century evil, the tanks, explosives, and machine guns that made their devastating appearance in the Great War, where he saw action at the battle of the Somme. Though Tolkien disliked mainstream modern authors such as D. H. Lawrence, he shared with many of them a demonizing of technology.

The fictional link between goblins and war machines goes back to "The Fall of Gondolin," a manuscript often alluded to in *The Hobbit*. In this work, written while Tolkien was recuperating from trench fever, a great elvish stronghold is overcome, not only by "dragons of fire" and "serpents of bronze," but by "things of iron that could coil themselves around and above all obstacles before them." These iron things carried goblins in their "hollow bellies" (*Book*, 2:177). The Trojan horse is reinvented here for a century that Tolkien saw as blighted by the worship of machinery. Another manuscript that predates *The Hobbit* describes goblins as creations of Morgoth, Tolkien's Satan: "The hordes of the Orcs he made of stone, but their hearts of hatred. . . . Goblins may they be called."[5] Tolkien's goblins are thus far from human, rather fleshy machines made from stone to serve evil.

Tolkien has often been accused of unrealistically polarized good and evil, and certainly the goblins represent a tendency to ascribe evil to entire groups. There literally is no good goblin but a dead one, and genocidal slaughter of three quarters of the mountain goblins at the end of *The Hobbit*, like a more wholesale slaughter in *The Princess and the Goblin*, means "peace" (245). The view here could be called medieval; like unconverted "pagans" in *The Song of Roland* and the shades of sinners in Dante's *Inferno*, goblins are creatures whose pain is occasion for moral pleasure. If Tolkien had thought thus about living people, he would have been a step away from Hitler. In fact, however, he did not confuse the moral clarity of his subcreated world with the ambiguity of the world in which he was a finite creature. And even in his subcreated world, where he saw into the deepest hearts of his characters, there are themes of free will and moral ambiguity. In a 1963 discussion of *The Lord of the Rings*, Tolkien attributes a conscience to Gollum years after his meeting with Bilbo and speculates what would have happened if the little monster had repented. This, he suggests, was always a real possibility, and Gollum's failure to repent is "tragic" (*Letters*, 329–30).

Between the flanks of good and evil defined by Elrond on the one hand and goblins on the other (a moral conflict emblemized by the ancient battle for Gondolin) most of the other characters waver, choosing poorly or well. Beorn, though on the *side* of good, might have sent Bilbo's companions away to starve in Wilderland had he not been humored (102), and the Wood-elves, like the men of Esgaroth, are cruel or helpful according to their selfish purposes. Bilbo and the dwarves, though defined as good when they oppose evils such as goblins or a dragon, are morally flawed, and their leader dies after being possessed by evil. Only Thorin's repentance repatriates him to the good side after greed has driven him into making war on the good men and elves.

Goblins, also called Orcs, are a special fictional case. Creations of the devil, unredeemably bad, they correspond to no actual persons or ethnic groups. They do symbolize corrupt urges that possess collective and individual wills. Thus, human beings, by abuse of free will, can become *virtual* goblins, though like Gollum they always retain some ambiguity, some potential for good. Goblins are, Tolkien wrote to his son during World War II, "only a figure of speech." There are no "folk made bad by the intention of their maker" (*Letters*, 90). Tolkien maintained a crisp distinction between the created world, where his knowledge was flawed, and the subcreated world, where he was omniscient.[6] He was haunted by a grim sense of evil loose in the world (*Letters*, 80), but he was no simple-minded moralist, and certainly no bigot.

I Have a Little Shadow

The still-childlike Bilbo must be carried by the dwarves as they escape the goblins because he is too small to keep up. Accidentally dropped, he is again alone and in danger, as he is at least once in every section of the story. Here is a basic childhood fear, fear of sudden abandonment, but it is precisely through episodes of abandonment and his mature responses to them that Bilbo grows. Later in the story, he will twice lapse unconscious in the midst of crucial actions, once in spider-infested Mirkwood and once in the midst of battle.

This particular device, losing consciousness and waking up in a new situation, is common in adventure stories and supports the interpretation of such stories as narratives of deepening consciousness. In the Babylonian tale of Gilgamesh, nearly four thousand years old, the hero is exposed as a mortal because he cannot stay awake, but he does receive divine wisdom through dreams. Unconsciousness is death's twin, but intervals of unconsciousness are steps in the climb to maturation. One-sided consciousness standing by itself, the Baggins side of Bilbo in *The Hobbit*, is stagnation: Bilbo grows by falling into the buried Tookish side and raising parts of it into waking consciousness. A stable and secure ego (as opposed to a rigid one) can entrust itself to the powers of unconsciousness in sleep, danger, or the creative process (Neumann 1973, 44). Heroes mature through "the sleep of healing, transformation and awakening" (Neumann 1963, 300). In hero stories there is a powerful link between the ability to dream prophetically and the ability to stay awake.[7]

The hero is often defined in terms of staying awake, maintaining consciousness, yet lapsing at fated moments of transition. Leadership is dreaming outside the boundaries of sleep. Bilbo saves his companions by staying awake and dreaming in the dry cave. Slow to sleep, he dozes off to a nightmare of goblins, then wakes and shouts a real warning. His alertness establishes new parallels between him and the hero of *King Solomon's Mines*. Allan Quartermain's Kafir name means "the man who gets up in the middle of the night, or, in vulgar English, he who keeps his eyes open" (Haggard, 47). Reluctant middle-aged guide on a suicidal trek with an old treasure map, Alan is also knocked unconscious in the midst of a fight (wearing, as Bilbo later will, protective chain mail of ancient make) (Haggard, 208). At a similar crisis in Haggard's *She*, the narrator faints,[8] and MacDonald's Curdie, trapped in goblin caves, falls asleep for hours (MacDonald, 99). Sudden unconsciousness covers difficult transitions in Jules Verne's *Journey to the Center of the Earth*, in "The Rime of the Ancient Mariner," and many other adventures, including *The Divine Comedy*, where Dante faints repeatedly. Bilbo is in good company.

Alone in darkness with only a knife, pipe, and tobacco—the same three articles with which Robinson Crusoe reaches the shore of his desert island[9]—Bilbo comes face to face not with Friday but with a dark side of his hobbit nature, a Hyde to his Jekyll. Gollum is identifiable with the part of the hero's personality that Jung called the shadow. This is not the same as the denied Took side of his personality, the side associated with adventures and elves. Even as the hobbit rejected a life of swords, mountains, and fireworks for himself, he admired it in others, and so Took traits suggest Bilbo's anima, his buried but beloved feminine side, associated with his mother and promoted by Gandalf. According to Jung's theory, the transforming power of the anima helps the conscious ego to meet and accept the shadow, which represents traits we dislike in others and are blind to in ourselves: "Such things as egotism, mental laziness, and sloppiness; unreal fantasies, schemes, and plots; carelessness and cowardice; inordinate love of money and possessions."[10]

The shadow, appearing in dreams as a human figure, represents traits we discarded to carve out a respectable identity early in life. Not all shadow traits are objectively bad; we become better, stronger people when we borrow some of the shadow's rejected powers. Though the shadow appears hostile, it may render valuable help, releasing hidden resources: Bilbo succeeds only through half-guilty use of the magic ring hoarded by his shadow. In fact, Jung repeatedly asserted that accepting the shadow (not acting out its raw impulses) is a prerequisite for achieving wholeness, the dynamic harmony of mind he called individuation.

Symbolism in the Gollum episode is strong. At a dead end in the roots of the mountain, symbolically the bottom of himself, Bilbo meets his double. Like Gollum, Bilbo lives underground, in tunnels, on a hill, at a dead-end, by water, and alone. Both creatures are resourceful, inclined to use cautious deception rather than violence, obsessed with food. Both are hobbits. The narrator in *The Hobbit* professes not to know what Gollum is (67), but in *The Lord of the Rings* Tolkien reveals that Gollum is a degenerate hobbit (that is, a human being) who stole the magic ring centuries before and has been corrupted by the ring even as it has extended his life span. Association between invisibility and moral corruption is central to H. G. Wells's *The Invisible Man*, which became a hit motion picture in the years *The Hobbit* was being written.[11] The Gollumlike character of invisibility coincides with recent writings on the subject of personality types. For instance, virtual invisibility is sought in real life by a personality type that Helen Palmer calls "the observer"—associated with social isolation, secretiveness, greed, and compulsive collecting.[12] It is easy to see in these traits of Gollum the shadow personality of the hobbit we met alone outside his obsessively dusted and arranged home with its full pantry.

When Bilbo spares Gollum's life, this should not be taken as pacifism. As Jung pointed out in *The Undiscovered Self*, where he analyzed the destructive projections of the Cold War, we must be very careful how we oppose shadow figures, carriers of our own denied evils. The compulsion to project internal evil outward and fight whomever it is projected on is a mental disease. In the presence of a shadow figure (once demands of self-defense have been met) understanding may be wiser than indignation. Thus Bilbo is right to spare his shadow, to leap over the crazed little figure rather than kill it. In *The Lord of the Rings*, Gollum, though disgusting and dangerous, plays a role in the service of the good. Like Judas, he becomes an instrument of salvation. To kill a shadow may be to drive it underground and increase its power, much as the attempt to crush German imperialism after World War I served to strengthen Hitler.

DARK WORDS

The riddle contest with Gollum shows how effectively Tolkien imitated Old Norse literature, where word combats with deadly outcomes are common. Snorri Sturluson's *Prose Edda* retells Norse mythology in the framework of a question contest between King Gylfi of Sweden and a figure named High One in Odin's court. Snorri's frame story is similar to Bilbo's encounter with Gollum. It tells of a mortal intruding into an uncanny place and being unable to "get out safe and sound" unless he wins the verbal combat by asking a question that cannot be answered.[13]

Norse combat of words, called *flytings*, typically involve swapping insults, as Beowulf and Unferth do in the Old English epic; but two poems in the *Poetic Edda* describe deadly quiz programs like Bilbo's encounter with Gollum. The *Alvissmol* describes Thor's questioning of a dwarf who wants to marry his daughter and who is destroyed when sunrise turns him to stone (Bellows, 184–94). More like Bilbo's contest is the *Vafthruthnismol*, which narrates Odin's visit to a giant's hall. His monstrous host declares: "Forth from our dwelling thou never shalt fare, / Unless wiser than I thou art" (Bellows, 70). To save his life, Odin propounds a series of questions, finally winning by asking a private question: What did Odin say in the ears of his dead son? With this, the giant recognizes his adversary and admits defeat (Bellows, 83). Like Odin's, Bilbo's "What have I got in my pocket?" (73) is a private question. And the *Vafthruthnismol* influenced a late saga that is another likely source of Tolkien's riddle contest, *The Saga of King Heidrek the Wise.*

Christopher Tolkien, a scholar and editor of his father's posthumous works, published a translation in 1960 of the saga bristling with parallels to his father's fantasy world. Most striking, however, is the younger Tolkien's claim that *Heidrek* contains the only Old Norse mention of a riddle contest, even of riddles (*Heidrek*, xix). The contest has much in common with the one between Bilbo and Gollum, for one of the parties is declared to forfeit his life if he loses the contest, and the threatened party wins by asking a private question, not a riddle. In the saga, Odin takes the identity of a mortal and visits Heidrek to challenge the wise king to a riddle match. After a series of riddles, Odin concludes with the same question he used against the giant in the *Vafthruthnismol*: he asks what he said in his dead son's ear. With this, Heidrek recognizes Odin and slashes at him with a sword. The god escapes, pronouncing a curse on the man (*Heidrek*, 32–44). Not only the presence of a riddle contest, with its nonriddle conclusion, but the sword and the curse pronounced on the winner (though roles are ironically scrambled) connect the two tales. In Wilderland the riddle contest is a sacred tradition (74), but the contest limited to riddles is imitated from one medieval European source only, *The Saga of King Heidrek the Wise*.

There are riddles, however, in Old English, and Tolkien's riddles owe to these. His remarks on the subject are ambiguous. A 1938 letter, celebrating his new status as popular author, suggests that there is "work to be done here on the sources and analogues" and wonders if his characters (hence he) will be allowed to claim authorship of the riddles (*Letters*, 32). A letter to his publisher nine years later, however, claims authorship of all but two of the riddles. They are original poetry in an old style and method, "literary" work not to be reprinted without permission (*Letters*, 123). These stances may not be contradictory if we recognize in the first a teasing celebration of the medieval tradition that informed his work and in the second an impulse to defend personal property.

The English literary riddle, the short poem describing an unidentified thing in accurate but misleading terms, begins with three collections of Latin riddles attributed to English churchmen around 700: Aldhelm, Tatwine, and Eusebius. Ninety-five riddles in Old English, a few translated from Latin but most original, appear in the largest manuscript of Anglo-Saxon poetry, *The Exeter Book*.[14] The riddle was well suited to Old English verse, which used many *kennings*, or riddling namings of things (the sea was a "swan-riding," for instance, and a ship a "flood-timber"), instead of metaphors or similes. Discussing kennings, Tolkien says that "the riddle element is present" but its purpose is compression, not confusion. "Even among the actual verse-riddles extant in Anglo-Saxon, many are to be found of which the object is a cameo of recognizable description rather than a puzzle." Though the Exeter riddles may perplex readers unfamiliar with their methods, Tolkien asserts, their purpose is literary in the fullest sense.[15] They should not to be confused with common jokes and puzzles. By Gollum's lake, Tolkien tries his hand at this long-neglected literary genre.

Bilbo's five riddles are not as interesting as Gollum's. The first, describing teeth as white horses, Tolkien acknowledges as traditional by saying "Gollum knew the answer as well as you do" (69). Bilbo's third riddle, describing an egg, is a condensation of a verse Tolkien credits to American nursery books (*Letters*, 123). Bilbo's fourth try, "No-legs," is traditional (a variation on the Oedipus riddle) and not in verse, and his winning question is, of course, not even a riddle. Bilbo's only riddle with literary claims is his second one, "sun on the daisies," a play on the word *daisy*, which was originally "day's eye" (*dæges eage* in Old English). The sun, too, is obviously "day's eye," and the little poem exploits this link. Tolkien's choice of riddles for Bilbo suggests an intellectual and literary lightweight, outclassed by the darker and more complex riddling of Gollum and saved only by luck.

Gollum's strong and memorable character is contained in his riddles, which loosely parallel several poems in *The Exeter Book* but are not translations. His lines read well aloud, as Tolkien once remarked (*Letters*, 164), but illustrators have found it difficult to capture the threat felt by readers (*Annotated*, 94). Although Gollum is small and man-shaped, the made-for-TV cartoon version by Rankin-Bass (1977), for instance, represents Gollum as a giant frog. This may be understood as a desperate effort to cartoon the sinister tone that Tolkien achieves through verses hissed under glowing eyes in the dark.

Gollum is terrifying because of the strength and perversity of his will, his mental depravity, shown through dark, densely written

riddles. *Mountain, wind, dark, fish,* and *time*—the solutions to his riddles—are elemental things that in Gollum's riddles take on monstrous
characters. If its elements are monstrous, the very universe must be
hostile. Gollum's riddles suggest paranoid depression. *Dark,* like the
riddler himself, is an invisible thing that hides under hills, destroying
"life" and "laughter" (70), and as harmless a thing as a fish sounds like
a cold and aggressive monster, invulnerable to natural limitations: in
silent armor, it is alive but does not breathe (71). The wind is similarly
monstrous; it cries, flutters, bites, and mutters (70). *Time,* for the little
long-lived monster under the mountain, devours, gnaws, bites, grinds,
slays, and ruins (72). What is so terrifying to Bilbo, and to the reader
with him, is that Gollum's riddles caricature in dreadful terms terrifying features behind pale eyes in the dark.

THE CONJUNCTION OF OPPOSITES

Just over the line that Tolkien's map labels "Edge of the Wild" (256) is
a realm of hybrids, creatures on borderlines between kinds. As mentioned earlier, goblins are man-shaped but not men; they are "stone"
copies devised by Morgoth, the Satan of Tolkien's mythology
(*Shaping,* 82). Gollum, too, is humanoid but of unknown species in the
text of *The Hobbit* (67), explained in *The Lord of the Rings* as an
ancient hobbit given longevity by the magic ring and adapted—in a
Lamarckian, not a Darwinian, way—to conditions of cave life. He is a
throwback to animal drives, a sort of hobbit cave man. The Wargs
blend species. They have language and government like human beings,
indeed like the skin-changing men described in *The Saga of the
Volsungs* who think like murderous men but look and speak like
wolves (*Volsungs,* 44–45). Tolkien's account of the attacking Wargs is
based on "The Battle of the Were-Wolves" in S. R. Crockett's *The
Black Douglas,* a story in which the leader of the wolves is a shape-
changing witchwoman (*Annotated,* 114–15). Besides being another
example of Tolkien's masculating characters who were female in his
sources, this clinches the implication that Wargs are semihuman and

should be associated with that familiar hybrid, the werewolf. Beorn's status as a creature between species is obvious.

Even the noble eagles evoke dozens of myths and fairy stories in which people take on bird cloaks to fly,[16] especially after they acquire golden ornaments. The chief eagle, Tolkien adds for no clear reason, later became the king of birds and "wore a golden crown, and his fifteen chieftains golden collars" (101). In Old Irish tales a golden ornament is an infallible sign that a bird is a human under enchantment. In one case flocks of birds linked with gold and silver chains are actually a princess and her fifty maidens.[17] A woman under enchantment is found in her swan-shape among many birds with chains around their necks (*Cuchulain*, 120). An immortal escapes with his love by transforming into swans "linked together by a chain of gold" (Gregory, *Gods*, 95).

Elrond, the elven man, was a transition into a land where creatures are double-natured, where opposites merge and connections are made. It is appropriate that here Bilbo meets his shadow and acquires the power of the ring, for the ring is a natural symbol of connectedness. It is associated with the primitive world-serpent biting its tail (the Ouroboros) and with the Mandala, the four-part circle that Jung saw as an image of healing. Like all round things, a ring suggests the self, the inner wholeness of personality that is obscured at infancy and is rediscovered gradually through the elaborate maturing process called individuation. The self is not a person's conscious identity, not the "I" represented by the hero, not the individual ego. The self, unless approached wrongly, does not make one "selfish." It is a complex of mental energy that, among other things, coordinates conscious and unconscious minds and is always centered below the edge of consciousness, where it takes on magical or divine properties. So Bilbo's ring, found in dark caves after sleep, will magically assist him in his efforts to become a whole person, a hero.

It is good to build a personality around the self, the process of self-development, or individuation. This is what Bilbo is doing in *The Hobbit*, prodded by Gandalf and others who are agents of the urge to wholeness. It is most important, however, for the hero who discovers the self, through whatever symbol, not to identify personally with it.

The danger, Jung wrote, "lies in the identification of the ego-consciousness with the self. This produces an inflation which threatens consciousness with dissolution."[18] Possessed by the idea of the self, a person becomes "inflated" by a chaotic inflow of raw energy, loses control, and becomes a tool of the infantile self, a golem. This is the danger facing Faustian dabblers in the occult or self-inflated leaders such as David Koresh and Adolf Hitler. This is what has happened to Gollum and what will happen to Thorin. Possessed by the self, they feel immortal and godlike and live in druglike animation, losing all moral proportion.

This same self is symbolically the Grail, the Christ, the World-Soul. Rightly followed, it is the way to fullness of life. The ring, if it does not possess the hero, gives him power to overcome the monsters of the subterranean world, the agents of the Great Mother who either initiates her children into adulthood or eats them alive (Gollum has been consumed by the ring and become a cannibalistic agent of the Devouring Mother). Bilbo's success depends, on the one hand, on his having the ring, his acquiring the connectedness with the self. On the other hand, it depends on his using the ring modestly, only when needed, remaining awake in his ordinary identity to resist temptation. As the protagonist in H. G. Wells's *The Invisible Man* says, invisibility gives a man the power to murder and terrorize,[19] but Bilbo instinctively uses the power within limits. Owning the ring causes him to grow into his real nature, to better fill his proper place, not to become twisted and alienated like Gollum.

The ring represents the unity of opposites—most obviously the union of Baggins and Took—and it is symbolically appropriate that it is found in Wilderland, the wilderness of bewilderment where creatures are hybrids of contradictions. The ring, as symbol of the self, links heaven, earth, and the underworld; spirit and matter; the conscious and the unconscious. It centers this panoramic episode in which Bilbo travels through the air and over and under the earth. He stands in inaccessible eyries, like Olympus in the clouds, and meets a dark double at the roots of a mountain. After the flamboyant synthesis of opposites in part 2, Bilbo will stand on his own as a hero. He has the ring and will not need Gandalf.

9

The Trek through Mirkwood

BILBO TAKES CHARGE

A new moral complexity enters the story in Mirkwood, the forest the dwarves must tramp through after they leave Beorn's house. Before this, the company was threatened by obvious villains—disorderly, quarrelsome cannibals who hated the sun—and took refuge with orderly and friendly nonhunters. In part 3, however, they are imprisoned by hunting elves fond of night who are nevertheless "Good People" (145). Indeed, the elves are perhaps better people than the dwarves. Corruption of Bilbo's companions, their own greed and suspicion, makes enemies of two potentially good groups, and later the same corruption will push them to the brink of war. Bilbo's dwarf companions are not by nature bad, as goblins are, but they begin in Mirkwood a program of bad decisions that almost destroys them. They suffer a vacuum of leadership that the hobbit fills. Led by Bilbo, the dwarves escape to take refuge with foolish men who themselves have corrupt leadership, men dwindled in the shadow of the dragon.

Dwarvish greed makes enemies of the greedy elves, and human greed welcomes the dwarves at the Lake-town.

In Mirkwood the good wizard is missing, and the only clear enemies are spiders. Bilbo must supply out of his own resources the cleverness and moral authority that Gandalf provided earlier. The hobbit must not only act bravely, which he has done before, but now for the first time he must chose wisely among ambiguities. He must act with discretion, tact, and cleverness. He must display not only courage but wisdom. The sword and magic ring won in his previous adventures are essential to his success, but they have limitations. Bilbo knows he must not hurt elves with his sword—he even feels guilty about taking their food (247)—and the magic ring can make only one person invisible (152). As suggested by the depravity of Gollum, the ring is as much a temptation to stagnation as it is a tool for escape and growth. Only wise and loyal tactical decisions give the hobbit a genuine advantage.

Part 3 echoes strongly the previous parts. Again the dwarves run short of food in "a gloomy tunnel," this time trees leaning over a narrow trail (123). Again they cross a body of water into danger. Again they run short of food and approach a fire at night, and again the result is that the dwarves (but not Bilbo) are trapped in bags while their captors argue about eating them. Once again Bilbo finds himself alone in darkness after having again lost consciousness, and again he uses his little sword to save himself. Once again a phantom voice prods villains into rash, self-defeating behavior and saves the dwarves from being eaten. Again the dwarves are captured, bound, and interrogated by a king in his underground throne room. Again the dwarves escape by an unusual means of transportation (in barrels, not on eagles), cross water, and are welcomed and promised supplies in a wilderness settlement where they are again not sure of their welcome, where they must again approach diplomatically. Again separated from the dwarves underground and in darkness, Bilbo again performs solitary acts of heroism and is rewarded. Part 3 is almost a repetition of the first two parts in compressed form and with different scenery.

The scenery is remarkably different, the forest hauntingly described and the giant spiders developed in a kind of sensory detail that the troll episode lacked. Perhaps the chief reason why thematic repetition does not feel redundant, however, is that this time the wizard is missing, and Bilbo must act in his place. When the hungry dwarves approach fires in the forest and stumble into trouble, as they did earlier, it is a Tookish Bilbo who engineers their escape. Having rescued them, he feels like "a bold adventurer," though he admits the advantage the magic ring has given him (143). The hobbit's reputation with the capricious dwarves is at its height, and he becomes their de facto leader in the absence of Thorin, their hereditary king. Again, after the dwarves have been captured by the Wood-elves, it is Bilbo who must perform the role of Gandalf and save them, and he does so with a cleverness worthy of a wizard.

Elves are immortal, dwarves stubborn and long-lived, so the standoff between the elves and dwarves might have gone on for years without his intervention. Thorin and Company might have been trapped behind magic doors, and the invisible Mr. Baggins trapped with them, skulking about and stealing food in a paranoid situation uncomfortably similar to Gollum's. Here again the hero is trapped under the earth, vulnerable to images of the Devouring Mother. Again, when the hero is not devoured, he graduates to a higher level of heroism, and the negative devouring force becomes a positive transforming one. Bilbo's solution, once he discovers the cell where Thorin is imprisoned, is to steal a key (a symbol already discussed) from a drunken jailer, free the dwarves, and pack them into empty barrels destined for the Lake-town down river. He falls invisibly into dark water after them. Here Bilbo is borrowing powers from his shadow, using the process of "bagging" (the specialization of monstrous foes prior to this), as a means of escape. So it is that the company, half-dead with hardship, enclosed and released again from things baglike, washes ashore within sight of the Mountain.

There are two *eucatastrophes* in these chapters, two turns in the action that would be happy endings if they were endings, but they are less sudden than earlier ones, such as the petrification of the trolls at sunrise or the swooping down of the rescuing eagles. They are less sudden because in part 3 Bilbo himself is the rescuer; he engineers the joyous turns, and so we see, step by step, how he operates. The second joyous turn occurs gradually as Bilbo finds the dwarves still alive in their barrels, then is given ceremonial form as townspeople acclaim Thorin King under the Mountain (169), followed by the usual consolations of rest, food, shelter, and song.

Unlike Elrond and Beorn, however, the Lake-men have lost their nobility under the shadow of the dragon. Absorbing the remnants of the old heroic town of Dale, they have degenerated into cautious merchants with a businessman for a leader, and this is not good in Tolkien's value system: "Commercialism," he wrote once, "is a swine at heart" (*Letters*, 55). Their leader is a selfish, cowardly pragmatist—a sort of Sir Kay without a King Arthur—who helps the dwarves only because his rabble demands it. Emblematic of the town's corruption is its location on piles in the river, a passive defense against the dragon. In the previous two parts, the company's passage over a river before reaching a house of refuge implied a baptismal grace, a barrier dividing

the house from the peril behind. But the Lake-town, midway in the river, offers no such grace. Ambiguity and moral irony, a tang of bitter satire very unlike the whimsy of the first chapters, appears toward the end of part 3, a tough sort of humor not absent from *Beowulf* and *The Odyssey*. The story, like its hero, is maturing and taking new risks on its journey east.

THE CONSCIOUS HERO

Bilbo succeeds because he progressively overcomes the stupor he showed in the first chapters, where he overslept, overate, and selectively forgot events such as inviting Gandalf to tea and agreeing to accompany the dwarves. In part 3 he is once more, like Allan Quartermain, "he who keeps his eyes open" (Haggard, 47), for he is again saved by waking at the right time. He notices small things and uses conscious willpower to control the impulses of appetite, fear, and despair. In this, he is contrasted with the dwarves, but especially with the overweight one, Bombur, who serves as a foil to show off Bilbo's maturing powers, a sort of corpulent minor shadow figure, a person who would rather dream than act. Bilbo, like Bombur, dreams of food and comfort but, unlike the fat dwarf, learns to accept suffering and take initiative. Bombur is one version of what Bilbo might have become had he rejected Gandalf and devoted himself to the well-stocked pantry back at the Baggins homestead.

Central to the testing of the dwarves and Bilbo in part 3 (a testing the dwarves fail, surviving only because Bilbo passes in spite of them) is the classic fairy-story prohibition. When Bluebeard's newest wife is told not to open a door, we know she will open it and suffer consequences. When Beorn and Gandalf tell the dwarves three times (the magic number) not to leave the trail in Mirkwood, we know they will leave it and suffer. The importance of "observing prohibitions," Tolkien wrote, "runs through all Fairyland" (*Tree*, 67). The motif is ancient, of course, going back as far as the forbidden fruit and Pandora's box, where an inability to resist breaking a mysterious rule suggests the innate sinfulness—or "flawedness"—of human will.

Nevertheless, the Christian doctrine of the fortunate fall, a theological commonplace familiar to students of medieval and renaissance literature, celebrates Adam's mistake. The death that Adam caused when he ate the forbidden fruit was "fortunate" because it allowed God to send a "second Adam," Christ, to redeem humankind (however painfully) at a higher level. The wrong choice, though still sinful, was right within a larger plan. Tolkien echoes this pattern in *The Hobbit*: like Adam, the dwarves suffer for their disobedience, but ultimately it deflects them onto the best path, the only open road, to their goal (164).

Still, this good outcome depends on the hero, the redeemer who makes higher choices. Unlike the dull and heavy dwarves, Bilbo grows in what could broadly be called spirit. He has the "sharpest eyes" (125), eyes that allow the dwarves to cross the black stream and that warn against their double-crossing Beorn (119). Even without using a magic ring, he is the lightest and quietest of the group, so that he is chosen to climb up into sunlight at the tops of trees (129). The magic ring is an extension of Bilbo's natural gift to see and notice without being noticed. Later—and most important—Bilbo's eyes and inquiring mind will discover the secret door into the dragon's Mountain, the secret keyhole in the door, and the one chink in the dragon's armor. Bilbo is not a Christ figure but merely a hero figure like Odysseus or Beowulf scaled down and made less physical. He does endorse the dwarves' appetite-driven decision to leave the road after their food has run out—agrees with Bombur, in fact. Nevertheless, once separated from them, he acts in an inspired and spirited manner: throwing rocks, singing, dancing, teasing, escaping, being where he is not expected, becoming a one-man army against the heavy stupid spiders, against whom the sluggish dwarves were helpless.

In his most spirited episode, saving the dwarves in Mirkwood, the invisible Mr. Baggins becomes a Puck, a Took, a trickster, a Peter Pan. Though hungry and miserable, he does the swashbuckling sort of thing he wished for back at Bag-End (22). He saves the dwarves, earns their respect, and becomes their leader. Even Thorin, a pompous hereditary king, defers to Bilbo. This might seem the culmination of all Tookish aspirations, the end of Bilbo's heroic development, but there is still an important element missing in his character, and to understand that, we should consider what Jung called the *participation mystique*, or mystical participation.

Jung defines the term to mean "an unconscious identity" (Jung 1969, 60). I am under the influence of a mystical participation when I act unthinkingly, that is unconsciously, under the influence of another person or group. The term *unconscious* is not to suggest that I am in a hypnotic trance, simply that I respond to the group's opinion and consider no other. I obey a collective will. Mob behavior is an obvious example of this phenomena, along with the compulsive force of fashion. The original mystical participation is the bond between mother and infant, the Edenic state in the first months of life before the infant learns that mother is "other." Individual identity comes into being with this first rupture of consciousness. The "I" begins with what is not mother.

Still, self-identity is fragile and easily falls back into participation with groups and ritual behaviors, political, social, religious, or professional. Indeed, Neumann argues in *The Origins and History of Consciousness* that early homo sapiens, even those in literate cultures, may have spent most of their lives sleepwalking in the mind of the tribe or family. The fully conscious, decision-making individual, identified with the hero who kills the "feminine" dragon of infantile participation, may be an anthropologically recent invention, only a few thousand years old. Ancient hero tales, which *The Hobbit* reinvents for the twentieth century, may celebrate a time when species woke up from the life of the herd.

The trouble with mystical participation is that the morality and taste of a single person is often superior to that of any group, especially if a person is "individuated" or has mature self-knowledge. Jung expressed it thorough the Roman proverb, *Senator bonus vir, Senatus bestia!*—"A senator is a good man, the Senate a beast." Unless he is an extraordinary leader, a man buries his strengths in a group rather than using them. He accepts choices he would never make on his own. Group action results in an "automatic lowering of the ethical level" (von Franz 1980, 196). A hero must learn to escape the undertow of consensus and rise to his own potential, bravely letting go of group support and the fuzzy comforts of participation.

To understand the process Bilbo undergoes, we should realize that people do not mature in isolation from a social group. The human being alone becomes like Gollum or the Invisible Man, freezing into infantile eccentricity; in fact, part of Bilbo's problem in the beginning is that he is too alone. He needs initiation into a male group, represented by the dwarves, to escape participation with his parent-haunted home at Bag-End and his generic hobbit habits. On the other hand, once he has escaped hobbit conformity through participation with the dwarves, he must escape the undertow of this new unconscious identity as well. He must not merely cease to be a dull hobbit by becoming a dutiful burglar, like men who use their jobs to escape their families but remain robotic in both spheres. Even as de facto leader of the dwarves (especially as their leader), Bilbo is absorbed into the group identity of Thorin and Company and has not become an individuated hero. To achieve this he must make hard choices on his own.

Individuation should not, however, mean leaving the group to become an outlaw (though some groups demand participation and outlaw members who become too conscious), but should mean substituting a voluntary affiliation for an automatic one. Marie-Louise von Franz describes the process: "It means on one side being less identical with the group, less melted into the group through *participation mystique*, and being firmer and more independently on one's feet; and at the same time it means being more consciously related."[1] Thus, though breaking a group bond feels like loss, betrayal, or failure, it should in fact be a "fortunate fall," a weaning away to prepare for new bonding at a higher level.

Katharyn F. Crabbe describes the process succinctly: "The paradox is that though he always moves *toward*, Bilbo is always gaining in confidence, competence, and character—all the qualities that lead to self-sufficiency" (43). Once recruited as the dwarves' burglar, he feels purposeless away from them, and leaves only when forced away. Each ordeal of return, however, reunites him with the dwarves at a higher level of independence, a strengthened ability to generate his own autonomous purpose. Of course, Bilbo's early success could be a trap, a temptation to stop maturing; he could freeze in the hero-leader stage and become not himself but a hero-image, a professional leader.

Bilbo's maturation is complete only when he becomes not an executive but a whistle-blower, so devoted to Thorin and Company that he is willing to be hated by them. The final paradox is that true loyalty includes the courage to oppose a group's errors and seem a traitor. The individuated hero may be worshiped or crucified—group responses distinct from his actual identity—and he must be willing to accept either outcome.[2]

A Gaggle of Analogues

For the educated reader Tolkien's fiction is tinged with recognition, not to say unoriginality. Dozens of references in "On Fairy-Stories" demonstrate that he knew well "the intricate web of story" (*Tree*, 20) where living tales and their shared motifs intersect and shine. He knew not only classical and medieval literature, fairy stories, mythology, and folklore, but the standard works of English literature, popular adventure stories, science fiction, and children's literature. His technique for weaving his own tales out of all this was apparently to let his unconscious lead, to write "visionary" fiction that symptomized his psyche, as distinct from psychological fiction.[3] When he composed, he felt he was "recording what was already 'there,' somewhere: not of inventing" (*Letters*, 145). In writing stories he semiconsciously mapped his mind (where else would the tales be "there") in the lines of old tales. His imitation was apparently dissociated from conscious intention. He claimed that, even when he wrote of Bilbo stealing a precious cup from a dragon just as the "thief" did in *Beowulf,* an obvious case of imitation, the Old English story or any idea of imitating it was not in his mind. Apparently, a precious cup simply seemed the thing for Bilbo to steal under the circumstances (*Letters*, 31).

So, even when we find a strongly similar older tale, an "analogue" to something in *The Hobbit*, we may not imagine the author mumbling, "Here's a good bit. I'll change it about and put it in." On the other hand, we cannot dismiss the possibility—even the likelihood—that he would not have written as he did without having read the older tale. Tolkien would not, for instance, have made a thief provoke a sleeping dragon by stealing a cup had he not read *Beowulf*, and so *Beowulf* is a clear "source." But many other tales may be only analogues, tales like others in a common stock that he drew from unconsciously as he wrote, so that even his guardian angel (he observed archly once) could not distinguish source from analogue, influence from accident (*Letters*, 288). Nevertheless, *The Hobbit* connects to other stories in the "intricate web." The influences are there, the analogues many. They suggest how Tolkien worked, and we need to look at some of them to sample the complexity of his debt to tradition.

Invisibility is a good place to start. Remembering that Tolkien was for years a student of classical languages, we may begin with the *Aeneid*, where Venus cloaks the hero in a cloud so that he can walk safely into Dido's palace. Siegfried in the *Nibelungenlied* has a *tarnkappe*, a cloak of invisibility.[4] Sir Thomas Malory's Merlin casts a spell of invisibility to save Arthur, and his Arthur's Balin slays "the marvelest knight that is now living, for he destroyeth many good knights, for he goeth invisible."[5] Finally, an actual ring of invisibility in Chrétien de Troyes's medieval romance *Ywain* allows the hero to hide from guards in a scene suggestive of Bilbo's "game" of blindman's buff with the goblin guards; also, Ywain is trapped, invisible, in a palace by a self-closing door much as Bilbo is in the palace of the Elvenking.[6] This analogue is interesting for two reasons, the visualization of the peril of an invisible man hunted by a group and the centrality of women in Ywain's story, the feminine again present in an analogue but purged from *The Hobbit*.

Though Tolkien's mythos has sent most critics searching for medieval sources, by far the best precedent for Bilbo's invisible escapades is the 1897 science fiction classic, *The Invisible Man*. His vulnerability and isolation, thieving food, and being blocked by doors and exposed to weather, betrayed by sneezing and wet footprints, and forced to sleep in uncomfortable places are natural consequences explored in detail throughout Wells's story. Tolkien knew Wells's work and mentioned it in his essay "On Fairy-Stories."

Tolkien copied the Wood-elves from more than an decade of earlier writings in which he counterfeited an Elvish history of the world.[7] These writings, the compilation of which he called the *Silmarillion* (*Letters*, 38), were sources for the "magic and mythology and assumed 'history' and most of the names" in *The Hobbit* (*Letters*, 21). So whatever traits of the elves come from traditional literature come secondhand, having passed through Tolkien's earlier efforts to create a mythology for England (*Letters*, 144). His elves resemble the tall traditional English fairies found in Spenser's *The Faerie Queene* and in Keats's "La Belle Dame Sans Merci," a folk unlike the insect-winged imps of later tales. The old Celtic tradition survives in medieval romances, but especially in Irish stories of the original folk of Ireland, the mound-dwelling people of the Sidhe. The above, however, are merely analogues, parallel strands in the web of tales, perhaps influential but no one a clear source.

One clear source, however, is the Middle English romance *Sir Orfeo*, which Tolkien translated into modern English many years before his death.[8] The harper-king Orfeo, modeled on the Greek Orpheus, mourns in deep woods after his queen is abducted by the king of Faërie. In the woods he begins to see beautiful knights and ladies, described as riding steeds "snow-white" like the deer that the dwarves meet in Mirkwood (*Orfeo*, 126; *Hobbit*, 127), and like Bilbo, he hears hunting and glimpses festivity by the folk of Faërie, and later discovers their habitation underground behind a magic door, a place he visits without being invited. Orfeo is not invisible, but he is in disguise. These are only general similarities, but Bilbo's first notice of elves in Mirkwood clearly echoes Orfeo's first notice of Faërie folk in his wood. In the Middle English, Orfeo hears a hunt "with dim cry and blowing, / and hounds also with him barking."[9] And Bilbo hears "dim blowing of horns in the wood and the sound as of dogs baying far off" (127). Once again, we recall that there are no women in *The Hobbit*, but women ride with the king of Faërie in *Orfeo*, a story centered on a man's love for his wife.

Bilbo's plan for escape from the Wood-elves' escape-proof cave seems synthesized from an odd variety of sources, conscious or not. The oldest is Homer's *Odyssey* (recall again that Tolkien was once a classics major), where Odysseus is similarly trapped in the cave of the

Cyclops.[10] Again motifs are scrambled but parallels are strong. In each scene, shut underground behind a stone door they cannot open, the hero and his followers seem trapped. The dangerous but clever solution involves drunken sleep, invisibility (for whatever reason), a nameless hero, and hiding in things that a door guard must allow out for economic reasons. The wine in both scenes is remarked to be of unusual potency and taste: in *The Hobbit* it is from Dorwinion, intended for the king's table, and in *The Odyssey* it is a gift from the priest of Apollo at Ismarus. And, finally, in both scenes the hero's most difficult problem is his own escape. Odysseus has tied two sheep together for each of his men and suspended the men under them, so the blind Cyclops will not notice as he feels the backs of the sheep leaving the cave, and Bilbo has sealed the dwarves in barrels. Odysseus clings under the lead ram, which attracts comment from the Cyclops by leaving last, and Bilbo grabs onto the last barrel thrown down into the underground river. Both heroes exit dangerously and last, but both are free throughout and release their bound companions once clear of danger.

Alexandre Dumas's *The Count of Monte Cristo*, a classic adventure novel of escape and treasure, has in its early chapters many analogues to *The Hobbit*, but especially the escape from the inescapable Château d'If when guards throw the hero Dantès into the water in a sack. The symbology of Jung and Neumann identifies this event, like Jonah in the great fish, as an expression of the Great Mother who kills and transforms. The fish protects as it traps, saves Jonah from drowning, but is itself a prison from which he must escape (like the ark of Noah, its analogue). We need only recall themes of death and rebirth in Christian baptism to glimpse the powerful symbolism that Tolkien invokes in Bilbo's watery underground escape into the sunrise. The dwarves, of course, are almost dead when Bilbo pries them out of their barrels, the tomb-womb vessels of their escape, and it is perhaps a lapse in the growing realism of his story that they are all alive. The actions of Dumas's hero explicitly symbolize death and rebirth as he strips and sews himself into a bag (bagging again) in place of a corpse, so that he is thrown into the bay outside the prison. Like Tolkien's laborers, men hauling Dantès's body comment on its weight—and the fall almost kills the man to whom it gives rebirth, as well as access to vast treasure.

Escape from a closed house through a trap door over water occurs in *Grettir's Saga*, noted earlier as a source of troll lore and a staple of *Beowulf* studies. A wife and her lover are trapped by her husband, who spies them through a window. The lover leaps into the sea through a secret trapdoor before the husband's friends can break in. The wife claims to have been alone (*Grettir*, 180). Of course, such intrigues would be out of place in a children's book, but here is yet another analogue, perhaps a source, contrasting with Tolkien's womanless world.

A very different work, A. A. Milne's 1926 *Winnie-the-Pooh*, suggests Bilbo's struggle to ride the unstable barrel on which he is floating down the river, which Tolkien elaborates in realistic terms (158–59). Pooh's escape across flood waters on the large honey jar he christens *The Floating Bear* is similarly eventful: "For a little while Pooh and *The Floating Bear* were uncertain as to which of them was meant to be on the top, but after trying one or two different positions, they settled down with *The Floating Bear* underneath and Pooh triumphantly astride it" (Milne, 128–29). The ironic understatement of this passage is underscored by E. H. Shepard's six small intertextual illustrations of Pooh's comic struggle to mount a barrel-shaped jar—illustrations that match Tolkien's words about Bilbo, "Every time he tried, the barrel rolled round and ducked him under again. It was really empty, and floated light as a cork" (158). At a moment of heroic victory, the struggle with the barrel undercuts Bilbo's dignity. Peter Pan becomes Pooh.

The range of analogues, some of them likely sources such as *Beowulf*, others perhaps only cousins of sources, suggests L. Sprague de Camp's comment that Tolkien was "one of those people who has literally read everything, and can converse intelligently on just about any subject."[11] His creative method, apparently mysterious even to himself, was to discover a story already in place in his mind and narrate it without self-conscious attention to its antecedents. The result is astonishingly original yet traditional, a juvenile book with wildly divergent roots in myth, children's literature, and centuries of adventure fiction.

10

Dragons Within and Without

Two Tales in One

The final two parts, or component tales, overlap at their joining so that, although the *eucatastrophic* pattern of the fairy story is maintained, there is no lapse of tension, no ceremony of tranquility like the ones that gave the other parts closure. Rivendell, Beorn's house, and the Lake-town are classic Homely Houses, sites of hospitality and joyful celebration, much as the Emerald City is for Dorothy and her friends. At these houses narrative tension all but lapses, and we might be at the end of a story except that a greater conflict projected in earlier chapters waits to be resolved. The *eucatastrophe* that ends part 4 is, of course, Smaug's crashing onto burning Esgaroth after the noble archer Bard shoots through the chink in his armor, a weakness Bilbo spotted. Because of a major flashback, however, an uncharacteristic shift in Tolkien's straightforward narrative, readers remain in the dark with Bilbo. We suffer the terror of believing that he is trapped underground; we share the suspense of exploring a treasure cave to which a dragon may return at any moment. Only after pages of shared suspense do we learn through the flashback that Smaug has been dead all along.

By the time Bilbo and the dwarves learn this—learn that they have, in fact, accomplished beyond all reasonable hope the stated mission of their journey—a new and ominous conflict is already on the horizon, the military plot of part 5. Thorin has become possessed by self-destructive greed, which Tolkien calls "dragon-sickness." A greed-crazed dwarf king, warped almost into a Rumpelstiltskin figure, has turned the smoke-stained palace under the Mountain into a fort, anything but a Homely House. In parleys with guests at his door, Thorin twists the language of hospitality into terms of violence and distrust, ignoring or belittling the natural bonds that should have led him to cooperate with others against the common enemies of goblins, wolves, and winter. Thorin, as dragonish king in conflict with men and elves, promises to be more deadly than the dragon that earlier slept in the Mountain. Thus, with a flashback, Tolkien passes the conflict ahead of the narrative line, blending the two closing tales into a single two-part movement of inexorable suspense.

The two overlapping final parts include eight chapters, two of which close the book with a grand procession of happy endings, visits to the earlier Homely Houses, and return home, all after danger has passed. But before this ceremony of consolation, Bilbo is progressively isolated from his earlier friends and followers, and he faces a series of dangerous and confusing tests. Also, he faces these tests in a less Tookish frame of mind than he had in Mirkwood, integrating the peace-loving character of the Baggins with the courage of the Took. This, of course, implies individuation, a stable escape from one-sidedness as the two sides of his character, still separate even during his earlier swashbuckling heroism, come together as one. He has not become possessed by the sword-wielding conventional heroism and confrontation that served him so well in part 3, but rather has dared to turn his back on it, to use his newly discovered courage in a gesture of self-denial and diplomacy. In part 4 he receives the armor of an elf-prince and, in cooperation with Bard, becomes a lower-case Sigurd, a dragon slayer. But in part 5 he returns bravely to the role of civilian thief, wearing the armor under his shirt and doing the right thing, even though he knows his friends will call it treason.

Thorin, his ego inflated by the hollow praise of the Lake-men, is once again king of the dwarves, and Bilbo's Tookishness is fading as the company enters the dragon's wasteland "at the waning of the year" (175). The dwarves characteristically lose focus, fall into Jungian participation, and wander away, antlike, from their secret door when Bilbo, observant and purposeful, notices that the hour of opening has come. Thorin's resolution has quickly faded, and Bilbo has again become the virtual leader. Again, he is the hero with open eyes: without him the dwarves' own Mountain would have remained shut to them, and once the tunnel is open, it is his job as burglar to investigate. Though Bilbo has a magic ring and is "a very different hobbit from the one that had run out without a pocket-hankerchief from Bag-End long ago" (183), his Baggins part wishes to be back home, and he becomes terribly afraid when he glimpses the fire of the sleeping dragon. Approaching its light, Tolkien declares, was his bravest act (184), a turning point perhaps second only to his finding of the ring. Bilbo must not only act bravely, but he must propel himself into a known and terrifying danger out of the abyss of a Baggins mood.

Bilbo, like the thief in *Beowulf,* steals a cup from the dragon, "a great two-handled cup" like those representing a woman-vessel with arms that Neumann sees as emblems of the Positive Mother, the symbolic antidote to the Negative Mother represented by a dragon (Neumann 1963, 120–23). Like much ancient and medieval literature, Tolkien uses a dream-vision to show a spiritual truth: the little hobbit appears in Smaug's dream as a hero "with a bitter sword and great courage" (186). Opportunistic and fickle like the sailors in Coleridge's "The Rime of the Ancient Mariner," the dwarves at first praise Bilbo for recovering part of their treasure, then grumble when the awakened dragon (like his double in *Beowulf*) discovers the loss and takes fiery revenge.

Huddled behind their door, Bilbo and the dwarves will soon again be swallowed up by the earth, again be promised starvation. The womb-door will close behind them, bagging them in the very tunnel they traveled for months to reach, apparently now their tomb. They are in the realm of the dragon, the Terrible Mother whose character it is to contain, ensnare, devour, and kill. Only by plunging through the center of her terror, going deeper into her mountain, can the hero evoke her positive character—she who contains, gives birth, develops, and rewards (Neumann 1963, 83).

As usual in the grammar of heroism, it is up to the hero with his symbolic sword—prominent in the restless dream of Smaug but apparently only a symbolic tool, for it plays no part in the dragon's defeat—to face the Terrible Mother with circumspection and bravery and work his own rebirth. This is something the dwarves, huddled in participation mystique and symbolically castrated, cannot even begin to do. We know that Thorin still has the elvish sword Orcrist because it ornaments his tomb after his death, as if emblematic of the nobility he regains through martyrdom (245), but during the crucial dragon-fighting episode, Orcrist is never mentioned. Even when Thorin does fight later in the Battle of Five Armies, he fights with an axe. Bilbo is the only sword bearer evident under the Mountain, a fact absurdly emphasized as he loosens his little sword just before confronting the gigantic dragon (183). The child-sized homebody that Gandalf recruited so many chapters ago is the only genuine hero is sight, the only one with the Odyssean potency of a blade.

In his second invisible visit with the talking dragon, Bilbo speaks in evasive language, imitative of Sigurd's conversation with Fafnir, "the prince of all dragons" (*Tree*, 41),[1] language like that used by Odysseus and Huck Finn to lie their way out of binds, and he succeeds as well as could be expected. Bilbo has matured since the troll episode and become a master of language as a weapon against evil, a clever Jack, though within the high moral ethos of Tolkien's world he deceives without actually lying. Though he inadvertently mentions the Lake-men and so provokes an attack on them (another fortunate fall), he shrewdly notices a gap in the dragon's armor, so that a Lake-man informed by a bird can slay it. Bilbo does his best, his very brave best, and events providentially fall into place, forming a good pattern in which even his mistakes are important.

At this point in chronological time, part 4 is virtually over, though the dwarves do not know it, and readers too are in the dark.

Once the dragon is killed all that remains is for the dwarves, led by
Bilbo, to find the courage to claim their hereditary halls and climb out
the great cavern door into sunlight, past ancient ruins to a watchhouse
where they rest, recover lost food, and notice birds gathering around
the Mountain. The dragon slayer—descended from a noble family of
Dale, the town at the gates of the Mountain—organizes refugees from
the broken Lake-town in the name of the selfish town Master. Soon,
joined by Wood-elves, Bard leads an army of men and elves toward the
Lonely Mountain. Their plans are to resettle Dale and—if Thorin is
dead, as they suspect—to claim and divide the treasure. This plan will
set them in deadly conflict with Thorin, who is suicidally inflated with
"the bewilderment of the treasure" (234).

The Curse of Treasure

Thus a new conflict is underway with surrogate dragons in human
form even as the dwarves hear of the death of Smaug. A prophetic
raven, very much like Mr. Raven in George MacDonald's *Lilith,* tells
Thorin, "The treasure is likely to be your death, though the dragon is
no more" (226). This prophesy echoes Fafnir's words to Sigurd: "And
that same gold will be your death, as it will be the death of all who
possess it" (*Volsungs,* 65). We should recall here that Fafnir himself
was once a man, that he had been transformed into a dragon by patri-
cide and greed.

   Once outside the Mountain, the dwarves are befriended by birds
who, like the nuthatches that address Sigurd (*Volsungs,* 66), volunteer
information and advice. The information is accurate and is used; the
advice is wise and is ignored. Thorin fortifies himself in the Mountain
and sends birds to call his cousin Dain to his aid. Bilbo becomes
increasingly depressed and alienated from the dwarves as an army of
elves and men camps outside the door and dwarves sing harshly to
drown out elvish music.

   Meanwhile, even as he defies an army outside his gate, Thorin
searches desperately for the Arkenstone, the hereditary gemstone that

is the heart of his Mountain. It is as if his dragon-sickness has two branches: (1) the self-inflated dream of holding the Mountain against an army and (2) the lust for the self-symbol that is the Arkenstone. Thorin, unlike Bilbo when he found the ring, cannot insulate his willful ego from the self, and its manic powers possess him. Inflamed to suicidal stubbornness by belief that the Arkenstone is near, Thorin would only become worse if he possessed it. So it is good that Bilbo, a little fellow of modest ego, finds the glowing stone by virtue of his bravery and sharp eyes, being first to walk past it on the dark pile of treasure. It is good that Bilbo has hidden the jewel in a bundle of rags: a public good but a private trouble, a temptation he must overcome or become like Thorin himself. The hobbit again reveals the ambiguous quality of heroism, its power to synthesize opposites: he feels the lure of the legendary stone but has courage to give it up, modesty to know it is not his. Nevertheless, clinging to it secretly, he can only surrender it for a reason.

That reason comes in a plan balanced dangerously between self-denial and megalomania: he proposes single-handedly to make peace by giving the Arkenstone over to Thorin's "enemies" so that the greed-crazed dwarf will be forced to redeem it by meeting their just demands. It is a bold plan, pulling together leadership qualities that Bilbo has been developing throughout the story, and Bilbo is presumably saved from megalomania—from inflation of his ego—by his humble return in rags to the dwarves rather than staying to be honored in the armor of an elf-prince. He would rather be a suffering servant among his own people than a triumphant traitor among strangers. He holds to his basic identity, Baggins from Bag-End, member of Thorin and Company, like the rare executive or politician who "remembers where he came from."

Repeatedly, since Gandalf left the party at the edge of Mirkwood, Bilbo has taken over the role of savior, of designated problem solver. Before, he was solving problems for Thorin, but now Thorin (inflated hollowly to kingly stature by the return to the Mountain) has become the problem to be solved. Bilbo's "betrayal" of Thorin, an ultimate escape from mystical participation and thus a move into individuation, is his last act as a substitute for Gandalf. It is perhaps unlikely that Gandalf would wait passively in the camp of the elves and men but not reveal himself until after Bilbo had completed his difficult mission alone, but this improbability only underlines the symbolic appropriateness of the story as it is told. If Bilbo had enacted his final heroism with Gandalf's encouragement, it would have become Gandalf's act, not the self-directed completion of a heroic character. Gandalf returns precisely when Bilbo has successfully enacted the Gandalf-role in his absence, when the hobbit no longer needs him. His return signifies that Bilbo has internalized within modest hobbit limits the powers of the wizard.

The irony, of course, is that Bilbo's modesty is founded in truth this time. He really is only a little fellow. The problem is really too great for him to solve, though his effort to solve it is a private victory. The higher moral in Tolkien's *eucatastrophic* structure is a Christian one. The finite efforts of the good are often inadequate to overcome evil, but the good must still persevere in faith, doing all they can within their limited vision without losing hope. Only when they have done their best is God likely to intervene through seeming coincidences that are manifestations of grace, such as the arrivals of Beorn and the eagles. A similar sense of the nobility of seemingly futile perseverance, in this case without assurance of a happy ending, underlies the ancient Norse ideal that Tolkien admired. E. V. Gordon, his friend and collaborator, put it thus: "The gods themselves knew that they would be overwhelmed by the evil powers, but they were prepared to resist to the last. Every religious-minded man of the heathen age believed that he existed for the sake of that hopeless cause."[2] Tolkien, emulating the *Beowulf* poet, makes his hero act simultaneously like a good pagan and a good Christian—like a good human being.

The rest of the tale moves swiftly. Thorin verbally agrees to meet the terms of his besiegers but reneges when an army of dwarf kinsmen arrives from the Iron Hills. A tragic "civil" war between the good seems inevitable. Then suddenly, in a sort of dark *eucatastrophe*, hordes of goblins and Wargs rush down under a cloud of bats. The bloody Battle of Five Armies begins. Outnumbered, the "good" armies at first have the advantage, then slip toward inevitable defeat, when Bilbo, clouded in invisibility but still sharp-eyed, looks skyward and is struck senseless as he shouts that the eagles are coming. Awakening from his third state of unconsciousness, he is rejoined in friendship with a dying Thorin, who has distinguished himself in battle and repented the bewilderment that transformed him into a virtual dragon.

The treasure is divided, with Bilbo expressing little interest in it but taking two small chests, and the journey home begins. Bilbo and Gandalf winter with Beorn, who arrived to turn the battle while Bilbo was unconscious, and they visit in the spring with Elrond. Near home, Bilbo breaks into original song, showing himself not the hobbit that he was (253), and finds that he has been presumed dead by his neighbors. In fact, he is reborn as new breed of hobbit, harmless to his neighbors but infused with a new freedom and joy in life, and appreciative of the friendship of elves and wizards. He has achieved the multisided child-like wholeness that is real maturity, life abundant.

A WILDERNESS OF DRAGONS

Under the fast-moving and transparent action of the final episodes teem literary traditions Tolkien understood so well that he was able to harness their powers without pedantry or open imitation. Compatible elements from a wide range of literatures rose up in his imagination and fused seamlessly as he recast them for the twentieth century. Such a complex—and again perhaps largely unconscious—literary process can only be hinted at.

Around the Mountain is the Desolation of Smaug, a wasteland that was once fair and green (173–74). It is the dragon's nature to hate living things, for he plans after burning the Lake-town to "set all the shoreland woods ablaze and wither every field and pasture" (211). As creator of desert, enemy of fertility, Smaug follows medieval precedents. Beowulf's dragon lives in a wilderness and flies out to burn houses, as does a fiery dragon in Gottfried von Strassburg's *Tristan*. Nithhog, a flying dragon in Norse mythology, gnaws at the roots of the tree that supports the world. In Edmund Spenser's Christian allegory, a dragon like Smaug in habitat and anatomical detail is an emblem for Satan. The fairy-story world Tolkien found "pre-eminently desirable" he defined by the possibility of dragons (*Tree,* 41), and his Smaug is an intricate synthesis of literary dragons, their habitations and treasures.

The most obvious source for Smaug is the *wyrm* in *Beowulf.* Both have lived unmolested for years in underground vaults and derived no benefit from their treasure. Both are angered by solitary thieves stealing precious cups while they sleep.[3] Waking, the *Beowulf* dragon smells the thief and angrily circles his hill, just as Smaug smells Bilbo, misses the cup, and hunts "round and round the mountainsides" (187). Frustrated, both dragons take generalized revenge by burning houses, including a great hall. Both spew flames and fly at night, hiding in their caves during the day, and details from the *Beowulf* description of the dragon attack—the gleaming approach, the firelight rising, terrified victims, the intent to leave nothing alive—all find their place in Tolkien's account.[4] Just as Beowulf is deserted by companions when he faces the dragon, so is Bard, and both dragons are subdued by wounds to vulnerable spots—Smaug in the hollow of the left breast, and the *Beowulf* dragon *niothor hwene* "somewhat lower down" (line 2699)—when attacks aimed at armored areas fail. Beowulf dies from the fight, and Bard is believed dead (213). Finally, the door to the *Beowulf* dragon's lair is a rocky arch through which runs a hot stream, like Tolkien's illustration of the "Front Gate" with its steaming river (174).

Smaug is, however, like so much in Tolkien, a synthesis of sources. Beowulf's dragon is a giant *wyrm* with a poisonous bite, a flying snake without human language or artificial armor, not as similar to Smaug as is the Old Norse Fafnir. In the *Saga of the Volsungs,* Odin (who often has birds sitting on his shoulders to tell him news) appears to tell Sigurd to thrust for Fafnir's heart from the underside, and the hero stabs "under left shoulder" (*Volsungs,* 63)—the same anatomical spot for which Bard shoots, instructed by a thrush. Both Sigurd and Bard use special inherited weapons, said to penetrate their full length; Sigurd's Gram enters to the hilt, and Bard's black arrow is buried completely in Smaug's chest, both presumably piercing to the heart. Also, Fafnir's treasure, like Smaug's, was originally owned by a dwarf, and Regin, a "dwarf in stature" intent on avenging his father, is the one who plans Sigurd's expedition (Bellows, 358ff). Of course, riddling talk and bird-speech are prominent in the Fafnir tale and in *The Hobbit* but are absent from the *Beowulf* dragon episode.

These two Northern dragons are giant snakes, however, and Smaug is represented by Tolkien as a classic heraldic dragon, with membranous wings, a doglike head, a snakelike tail, four birdlike claws, and a body covered with spines and scales. Such a monster is on the heraldic badge of Wales and associated with British royalty. Indeed, Smaug's lizard shape, red-golden hue, and jewel-mail recall a flying dragon in a dream of King Arthur from Malory's *Le Morte D'Arthur:* "his shoulders shone as gold, his belly like mails of marvelous hue, his tail full of tatters, his feet full of fine sable, and his claws like fine gold; and an hideous flame of fire flew out of his mouth, like as the land and water had flamed all of fire" (1:134–35). Smaug, too, makes the lake "red as fire" (210), and his character is regal if malign. He is, as Tolkien ironically points out, King under the Mountain.

But the closest model for Smaug's appearance is the dragon the Red Cross Knight slays in book 1, canto 11 of *The Faerie Queene,* which is huge like Smaug and creates stupendous effects around him, a much more formidable opponent than the horse-size dragons in traditional illustrations. Beyond the standard heraldic features, Spenser's dragon has Smaug's glowing eyes, uses his tail like a flail, and has vast, noisy wings. He is armored

> Like plated coate of steele, so couchéd neare,
> That nought mote perce, ne might his corse be harmd
> With dint of sword, nor push of pointed speare.[5]

Once again, the dragon is hurt by stabbing the vulnerable spot under his left wing, a blow that saves the hero, though it does not kill the dragon. A thrust to yet another vulnerable spot, the mouth, slays Spenser's satanic emblem "so downe he fell, and like an heapéd mountaine lay" (138).

Smaug's hoard includes jewels, silver, gold, mailcoats, helmets, axes, swords, spears, harps, a cup, and a necklace, most of which are found in the *Beowulf* cave, perhaps the most complete medieval inventory. Bilbo, like Sigurd, rides away with two chests of treasure and a mailcoat from the mountain of dragon-treasure (*Volsungs*, 66). The light silver coat that protects Bilbo resembles fine-woven shirts in Norse sagas,[6] and especially a mailcoat of tiny triple-woven silver in Chrétien de Troyes's *Eric et Enide,* light as a silk jacket.[7] If there is a single literary precedent, however, for Bilbo's elf-prince mailcoat, it is Victorian, not medieval, the heirloom "magic coats" of chain armor normally worn by royalty but lent to Quartermain and his friends in *King Solomon's Mines.* These coats, though less ornate than Bilbo's, are "the most beautiful chain work we had ever seen. A whole coat fell together so closely that it formed a mass of links scarcely too big to be covered with both hands" (Haggard, 157–58). Of course, both heroes receive armor as gifts after deadly journeys to fabled kingdoms of treasure and peril. Haggard's hero wears chain under his ordinary clothing, as Bilbo and the dwarves do (204), and both heroes are armored in battle scenes that soon follow.

The plan used against goblins in Tolkien's Battle of Five Armies is good military strategy, a classic pincers movement taking advantage of high ground, perhaps reflecting Tolkien's World War I officers' training. Haggard's fictional battle, however, follows almost exactly the same plan on similar terrain: Bard and his allies draw the goblins between two barren spurs of the Mountain and attack down onto their flanks from those spurs, while Ignosi draws his enemies between the arms of a rock-strewn "hill curved like the new moon" (Haggard, 175). Both battles involve a feint of defending the low ground between two arms of high ground, a suicidally brave move necessary to set up the pincers, and then an attack down from the arms once the enemy has won the ground between. Both battles involve reverses and tremendous carnage, piles of bodies, and at one point a small ax-wielding cadre of heroes surrounded by a sea of enemies (*Hobbit,* 240; Haggard, 223), and there are many other similarities.

In both books, for instance, the narrator stands in the thick of the fight but avoids fighting, an alien in the midst of a strange but admirable army. Knocked senseless at a desperate moment, he is later told the outcome of the battle (*Hobbit,* 240–45; Haggard, 207–10). Both battles are decided by giant fighters compared to Norse berserks and functioning like Homer's Achilles. In *The Hobbit* it is, of course, Beorn, the shape-shifting bear-man, whom "nothing could withstand" (244), and in *King Solomon's Mines* Sir Henry, nicknamed the Elephant, mows down enemies "like his Berskir forefathers . . . till at last none would come near the great white 'tagati' (wizard), who killed and failed not" (Haggard, 226). Battles in both works begin in darkness and siege and end in sudden rout. The art of battle narrative is ancient, as old as the *Iliad,* but Haggard was a master of the art in novelistic style, accused by an 1892 reviewer of "rejoicing in cruelty, revelling in carnage" (Haggard, xvii), and Tolkien learned much from him.

There are also many touches of Haggard, overlaying *Beowulf* of course, in Smaug's treasure cave. Like Tolkien's dwarves (and Voltaire's Candide outside Eldorado, incidentally), Quartermain stuffs his pockets with jewels from the treasure cave (*Hobbit,* 203; Haggard, 292). In both stories a massive gem is the heirloom of the king ruling the mountain. In both stories, a bat startles an adventurer by flying in his face in an underground hall of the dead (*Hobbit,* 202; Haggard, 262). In both stories a party of outsiders, helped by local people but sent in alone, are trapped by a door of heavy stone, "buried in the bowels of a huge snow-clad peak" (Haggard, 286). No dragon, but analogous to the dragon—especially the dragon as Terrible Mother—is the blood-thirsty, centuries-old witch Gagool, guardian of Solomon's treasure, explicitly reptilian as she traps Quartermain's party: "she crept, crept like a snake out of the treasure chamber and down the passage toward the massive door of solid rock" (280). On the previous page she is like a bat. The value of food and water over treasure is stressed in both accounts. Trapped a second time with treasure, Tolkien's dwarves are told, "We will bear no weapons against you, but we leave you to your gold. You may eat that, if you will!" (224). And Haggard's Gagool mocks Quartermain's party, "There are the bright stones that ye love, white men, as many as ye will; take them, run them through your fingers, *eat* them, hee! hee! *drink* of them, ha! ha!" (276).

There are more parallels, but again motifs are organically reassembled, fused into a new story by imagination, so that *The Hobbit* cannot rightly be called a retelling of *King Solomon's Mines,* any more than of *Beowulf, The Wind in the Willows, The Odyssey, The Invisible Man, Don Quixote, The Count of Monte Cristo, The Princess and the Goblin,* or *The Saga of the Volsungs.* Nevertheless, its theme of heroic quest is informed by these works and many others, a tripart tradition quite alien to modernist fiction and one that Tolkien breathed new life into for his own time. And causally, *unconsciously,* if we are to believe his own accounts of his method, he explored the traditional theme of a hero's quest for individuation through a complex but graceful synthesis of hints and outright imitations from traditional epics, nineteenth-century fiction, and recent children's stories, all of it infused—and here was perhaps his most personal contribution—with a sense of the history and powers of language.

11

Languages of Naming

NAMING BY CAPITALIZATION

The great Icelandic writer Snorri Sturluson, on the first page of his introduction to Norse mythology, tells how four oxen from Giantland (uncles to the Blue Ox in the genealogy of tales) plowed a gigantic furrow that filled with water and is known in Sweden as The Lake. Here, at the head of a medieval work from which Tolkien derived the names of his dwarves, is the principle by which he derived many other names.

A child living in a house with a street in front and a field in back speaks to Mother of the House, the Street, and the Field, as surely as Christopher Robin's rabbit is Rabbit and Mole's wild wood is the Wild Wood. Tolkien points to this kind of naming when Bilbo asks Gandalf why the stone hill near Beorn's hall is called the Carrock. Gandalf answers, "He calls things like that carrocks, and this one is *the* Carrock because it is the only one near his home and he knows it well" (102). This sort of naming is universal. Americans call their south (which is north of most places) the South. When Bilbo (from The Hill overlooking The Water) journeys to the Mountain by the Long Lake, Tolkien is naming in a familiar way.

There are advantages to such naming. Obviously, it makes for easy reading and fewer hard words. This alone is a step down a slippery slope to "See Jane run," but balanced with other strengths, still an advantage. *The Hobbit* is a classic bedtime book, and when Tolkien wrote the sequel with its multilayered, opaque names, he knew he overshot his younger audience (*Letters,* 24).[1] Also, naming by capitalization immerses us in a worldview where home is the center of the universe and we are ignorant of larger landscapes that would require our hill to be anything but The Hill. This is Bilbo's initial worldview, an Edenic one to which we can all return in imagination. On the first page we meet a simple country squire in his home in "the side of the hill—The Hill, as all the people for many miles round called it." Tolkien uses familiar objects such as tea, mince-pies, and clocks on mantels, anachronisms in Middle-earth, to cleanse Bilbo's home of virtually that strangeness (for 1930s middle-class British readers anyway) that poststructuralist critics call the "other." The hobbit (unnamed for almost two pages) is a middle-class Everychild, prosperously grown up but otherwise unchanged; and his home, though underground, is familiar to its intended audience: "real" despite its place on the edge of a subcreation of elves and dragons.

Readers accept Bilbo's home as a point of departure because its names are familiar, so they will later suspend disbelief easily when, with Bilbo, they leave this comfortable center and find monsters and marvels "out there." This effect is important to Tolkien's art. Even in *The Lord of the Rings,* names of hobbits and their home shire are anglicized to create a familiar point of departure, and lengthy initial chapters linger in hobbit lands. Plain English is used to establish acceptance and belief.

For hobbits, who seldom travel more than an afternoon's walk from home, naming by capitalization is a sign of provincialism; but in the well-traveled dwarves, it signifies something else. The dwarves' fixation on their lost home makes a mountain hundreds of miles away *the Mountain* and places around it the Long Lake, the Lake-town, and the Withered Heath. The diaspora of the dwarves has created a second center of the universe, one projected many miles away by legendary history and family honor. Their experience has two centers, where they are and where they came from. Here is the skewed provincialism of refugees for whom the Mountain is not a place that people call "the Mountain" for miles around, but a remote mother peak most of them have never seen—yet a clear reference despite the fact that they must traverse a range of mountains to reach it. Between the Hill and the Mountain, two centers marked by capitalization, there are opaque, foreign names.

In a note to his lecture "On Fairy-Stories," Tolkien celebrates literary fantasy. Words evoke the primal places of each reader's heart. "If a story says 'he climbed a hill and saw a river in the valley below,' . . . every hearer of the words will have his own picture, and it will be made out of all the hills and rivers and dales he has ever seen, but especially out of The Hill, The River, The Valley which were for him the first embodiment of the word" (*Tree*, 80). The language here is Christian, sacramental. It speaks of incarnation, both the word made flesh and the divine creative word. Tolkien scribbled "In a hole in the ground there lived a hobbit" on a blank examination page some time before 1930, and with those words an age of Middle-earth began. What hill could the hole be in but The Hill?

NAMING DWARVES

The pre-Christian myths of Northern Europe—stories of Thor and Odin, dwarves and dragons—survive almost entirely through the literature of Iceland, settled after 870 by aristocratic refugees from Norway. Icelanders, a close-knit population, retold stories of ancient gods and Viking heroes. When Christianity came to the island in 1000, pagan vernacular poems (once the shared heritage of the North but suppressed elsewhere) were recorded in the script of the missionaries. The language, a branch of the Germanic family, is today called Old Norse. The earliest Icelandic collection was edited in the twelfth century by a scholar named Saemund and survives in one manuscript (lost for centuries) called the Codex Regius. Until it was found, the myths in Saemund's *Poetic Edda* were known from paraphrases and quotations in Snorri Sturluson's thirteenth-century *Prose Edda*. Snorri's work remains valuable because he understood the old traditions and wrote to explain them to a new generation. Together the two "Eddas" are a window into an ancient Germanic mythology that would otherwise have been all but lost.

As a child Tolkien loved the Eddic tale of Sigurd the dragon slayer, retold in Andrew Lang's *Red Fairy Book* (Carpenter, 22). While still in preparatory school, he studied Old Norse and delivered a paper about sagas, quoting in the original language (Carpenter, 49), and at Oxford, he chose Norse as a special subject (Carpenter, 63–64). With E. V. Gordon, author of the standard *An Introduction to Old Norse,* he founded a club at Leeds University dedicated to reading and singing Norse literature (Carpenter, 105). Tolkien proudly emulated Norse heroic literature in his fiction.

Most obvious is the naming of his dwarves. The *Voluspa* in the *Poetic Edda* tells of the creation of the dwarves (*dverga*) and lists their names. The list is gibberish to readers today, but seemed so important to Snorri that he quoted and expanded it. The dwarves, he says, quickened like maggots in the flesh of Ymir, the giant whose corpse is the earth. From the gods the dwarves took human shape and mind, but still lived in stones underground. Snorri's catalog (here transliterated into modern alphabet) lists nearly all Tolkien's dwarf names and *Gandalf*:

Nyi, Nithi,
Northi, Suthri,
Austri, Westri,
Althjolf, *Dwalin,*
Nar, *Nain,*
Bifur, Bafur,
Bombor, Nori,
Ori, Onar,
Oin, Mothwitnir,
Wig, ok [and] *Gandalf,*

Windalf, *Thorin,*
Fili, Kili,
Fundin, Wali
Thror, Throin . . .
Hlethjolf, *Gloin,*
Dori, Ori . . .
Eikinskjaldi. (Sturluson, 15–17)[2]

Only *Balin* and *Thrain* are missing, and *Thrain* appears in Saemund's list.[3] The last name in the list, literally translated, appears as Thorin's second name, Oakenshield.

In the ancient religion of Northern Europe, *dverga* represented elemental forces of nature, ageless and deadly. They crafted magical objects, were invoked in charms, and resembled goblins. In contrast, Tolkien's fictional dwarves are a natural flesh-and-blood race, human in their goodness and corruptibility. Still, they keep many traits associated with the forces the Norse *dverga* symbolized: dwelling underground, extraordinary craftsmanship, stubborn wills, and long memories.

Gandalf, meaning literally "wand-elf" or figuratively "magic elf," is explainable as a description capitalized into a name in the centuries-old dialect that Old Norse represents in Tolkien's hobbit fiction (Gandalf is centuries old). Tolkien's first handwritten draft called the wizard *Bladorthin,* the chief dwarf *Gandalf.* Comical and unpleasant associations are enough to explain dropping *Bladorthin* and returning to the dwarf lists for the name *Thorin.* Later Tolkien recycled *Bladorthin* to name an Ozymandiaslike king whose treasure is in the dragon's cave.[4]

OTHER NAMING FROM THE GERMANIC

As T. A. Shippey explains in his ground-breaking discussion of Tolkien's "asterisk-reality," nineteenth-century philologists such as Jacob Grimm were able to construct rules that charted shifts in pronunciation as the great Indo-European family of languages, and particularly its Germanic branch, evolved historically. A given word in Old Norse, Gothic, or Old High German takes a more or less predictable form in English at a given time and place. The English word is predictably different from its Norse cousin; its form may be derived with confidence by applying rules for sound change that by 1900 were established as the basis of the science called *comparative philology* (Shippey, 15–18).

Tolkien illustrates this in his introduction to John R. Clark Hall's translation of *Beowulf*. The word *hose,* he points out, appears only in that poem, nowhere else in English, but its meaning is clear. By the rules of grammar and sound change, *hose* is the "same" as Old High German *hansa,* meaning "retinue" ("Prefatory," xii). By such methods philologists construct how words recorded in one language would have been spelled had they survived in another language. The convention is to mark such words with asterisks to distinguish them from words actually recorded in manuscripts.

Asterisk words are not empty fabrications; given the scarcity of surviving manuscripts, many asterisk words must have actually existed in speech or in manuscripts now lost. *Hose* would be an asterisk word if the *Beowulf* manuscript had burned (rather than being lightly scorched) in a 1731 fire at the Cottonian Library, and clearly other fires have exiled living words into the limbo that Shippey calls "asterisk-reality." In this limbo are jumbled words that were and words that might have been, visible only to scholars adept at the laws of sound change. Not only are asterisk words there, but asterisk societies and asterisk histories that would have preserved and used these words. This is heady business, hypothetical as theoretical physics, accessible only to those who have paid their dues with years of study.

Tolkien was a fan of science fiction (*Letters,* 377), and philology was his science. He sat "at the feet of" Joseph Wright, the great Max Müller's successor to the chair of comparative philology at Oxford (*Letters,* 397). When Tolkien first studied under Wright, the German-educated Englishman had edited the six-volume *English Dialect Dictionary* and published primers of Middle and Old High German and Gothic and comparative grammars of Old English and Gothic.

Wright's rigor and Tolkien's own love for words awoke in the young student the romance of philology, not as a collection of rules but as a matrix of lenses through which he could view the asterisk worlds implicit in words, worlds past and worlds possible. Tolkien mastered comparative grammar, but he didn't write grammars. (He did proof-read the grammar section of Gordon's *An Introduction to Old Norse*.) What Tolkien wrote was criticism informed by philology—and, of course, poetry and fiction set in asterisk worlds of philological science. A good example of how language shaped his vision is the character built around the Old English word *beorn*.

Let Tolkien himself explain the word. *Beorn*, he writes in an introduction to *Beowulf*, is a poetic word meaning "warrior" or "man," a word never used in ordinary speech to refer to men. It was an obsolete form of the word *bear* (which had already evolved to *bera* in Old English), a form recorded as *biörn* in Old Norse ("Prefatory," xvii). A *beorn* was a man with the attributes of a bear, much as a predatory man today is called a wolf or shark. The archaic form of the word shows that it existed for centuries in the language of heroic poetry and, like the tale of Beowulf and the Danish king, had been imported to England. If we follow the philological trail back through Beowulf, *beorn of beorns*, we learn what it means to be a bear-man.

To begin with, "Beowulf" may be a synonym for "bear." As early as 1854 Jacob Grimm interpreted the name as a kenning (a type of metaphorical compound) meaning Bee-wolf, or foe of bees. (This is, of course, asterisk reality, for no such kenning is in any manuscript.) Strangely, Grimm read Bee-wolf to mean woodpecker, noting that classical mythology praises the bird's courage and that woodpeckers eat bee larvae. But most scholars support the obvious interpretation: a bee-wolf is a bear, a creature respected for its strength and reputed human intelligence in the regions where the tale of Beowulf originated, a creature regularly described by kennings referring to honey (Chambers, 365–66).

Tolkien was aware of this hypothesis. Not only is it elaborated for pages in R. W. Chambers's landmark *Beowulf: An Introduction*, published in 1921 and revised in 1932, but is discussed in Klaeber's edition of *Beowulf*, standard since 1922.[5] These were basic tools of

Tolkien's trade. Chambers takes on all opposition, not only arguing that the hero's name means "bear" but connecting the tale to similar monster-fights by bearlike heroes, particularly one Bjarki ("Little Bear") whose father was turned into a bear by enchantment (Chambers, 369). Chambers's discussion of *Beowulf* as a literary variant of the Bear's Son folk tale (62–68) is at least one of Tolkien's targets in "On Fairy-Stories" when he declines "to discuss the turning of the bear-boy into the knight Beowulf" (*Tree*, 29). Beorn springs not only from the word *beorn* but from the bear-boy myth.

The compound "skin-changer" in *The Hobbit* is a piece of creation by philology. It translates Old Norse *hamrammr*, which refers to the state of warlike fury of the *berserkr*. The latter term, barely altered in spelling or sense since it migrated into English, refers to ancient Scandinavian warriors who fought with wild fury, who went "berserk" in battle. Tolkien knew that *berserk* was derived from a compound of roots meaning "bear" and "shirt." A warrior goes "bear-shirt" by wearing the pelt of a bear, thus changing his skin. Tolkien's philologist son Christopher explains: "Berserks were said to fight without corselets, raging like wolves with the strength of bears, and might be regarded almost as shape-changers, who acquired the strength and ferocity of bears" (*Heidrek*, 93). Remove the "almost," and you have a description of Beorn in battle: "He came alone, and in bear's shape; and he seemed to have grown almost to giant-size in his wrath" (244). Unarmed but protected by his bearskin, Beorn slaughters wolves and goblins with sheer animal strength, much as the bear-boy Beowulf, "the strongest of mankind," kills Grendel when swords and armor have failed.

Early in Snorri's *Heimskringla* is an episode strongly suggesting the Beorn episode in *The Hobbit*. After the murder of her husband, Queen Astrid takes refuge in a holm (from Old Norse *holmr*, a small island in a lake or river). Leaving this island, pursued by assassins and disguised in "mean clothing," she and her party beg a night's lodging from a rich but inhospitable yeoman named Biorn, whose hall is "east of the mountains."[6] Here, in a small space, are analogues not only to the name but to the mountains, the goblin pursuit, the Carrock, Bilbo's painful awareness of his "many missing buttons" (105), and, of course,

Beorn's inhospitality, which Gandalf overcomes by means of a charade. Tolkien recalled an attack of writer's block after Thorin and Company were rescued by the eagles, just before they met Beorn (*Annotated*, 1). And in this cluster of analogues is circumstantial evidence that Snorri's history (colored by asterisk realities evoked by *beorn, Beowulf, berserkr, hamrammr,* and *holmr*) gave him the jumpstart he needed.

Beorn's Wilderland is an asterisk-place constructed from philological ideas. In a part of *The Hobbit* dominated by wer-beings (Elrond is an elf-man, goblins devil-men, Wargs wolf-men), Beorn develops the equation between man and bear. If a man had ursine stature and character, he might be large, strong, solitary, short-tempered, and violent. He might be vegetarian and fond of honey (which he would cultivate), harmless to livestock (which again he would cultivate), and almost maternal in his defense of his "den" and his "children" (including people adopted through the sacred guest-host bond). In his bear-man state, he would not fight with weapons and, by extension, might avoid metal as far as humanly possible, using only the woodman's axe to construct his hall, hives, and gate.

Beorn's hall, as drawn by Tolkien, obviously imitates the Old Norse hall in E. V. Gordon's *Introduction to Old Norse* (28) except for the absence of weapons, presence of log-section seats, and differences in carvings. The upper columns in the Norse hall are carved into totem-pole-like human figures, inappropriate to the animalized solitary, whose posts branch like trees, rendering the hall a symbolic forest. As bears haunt woods and are kings of the (northern) forest, so the man-half of the bear-man is as much forester as warrior. Beorn will become "a great chief" of the woodmen after the goblins are defeated in the Misty Mountains (248).

Carrock, Beorn's word for a stone in the path of the Great River, is a term that might have survived into standard modern English. The word suggests Old English *carr* ("stone") and Gaelic *carraig* ("a headland, a cliff, a rock jutting into the sea"). The *Oxford English Dictionary* (OED) lists *carr* as still in use for rock islands off the Northumbrian and Scottish coasts. If *carraig* existed in modern English, it might have been affected by a linguistic process called "folk

BEORN'S HALL

etymology," which respells unintelligible foreign loan-words to include intelligible native elements. Folk etymology respells to invent word histories that "make sense."[7] If *carraig* ("rock") had entered common English, it might have become *carrock* by the same logic that French *crevisse* became *crawfish*. In fact, along the Scottish border it may have. Joseph Wright, Tolkien's teacher, lists *carrock* in his *English Dialect Dictionary* as the Northumbrian spelling for a term that in northern England means "a heap of stones used as a boundary mark, burial place, or guide for travelers." The Carrock is this too: it marks the boundary of Beorn's territory, and Gandalf and the eagles guide their travels by it. So Beorn's Carrock is a Gaelic *carraig* and a Northumbrian *carr* and *carrock,* a philological concoction with a likely nod to Joseph Wright.

J. S. Ryan's 1966 "Germanic Mythology Applied" seemed at the time to learnedly decipher scores of Tolkien names, including *Smaug* as a form of Old English *sméocan* ("to emit smoke").[8] But Smoky the Dragon is the sort of guess Tolkien condemns when he calls the article "nonsensical." Ryan, he says, did not understand how philologists go about inventing language (*Letters,* 380). Ryan ignored rules of sound change, the steel heart of philology, according to which rules *Smaug* is not "the same as" *sméocan.* In fact, Tolkien explained as early as 1938, it is "the past tense of the primitive Germanic verb *Smugan,* to squeeze through a hole; a low philological jest" (*Letters,* 31). Readers may at this point feel helpless before the professor's arcane learning; we could not have caught the joke on our own. Still, once explained, it is critically useful. Linking Smaug with smoke told us nothing, but a jest about hole-squeezing authorizes, intentionally or not, readings that develop symbols of birth and rebirth, even sexual readings. As Freud showed in *The Psychopathology of Everyday Life,* we give ourselves away with humor.

Similarly helpful is the naming of the Wargs, whom Tolkien calls "an evil breed of (demonic) wolves." The term is a "Germanic form as representing the noun common to the Northmen" (*Letters,* 381). Old High German *warg* (cognate of Old English *wearg* and Old Norse *vargr*) is spelled as the root might have been spelled had it survived in modern English—related to the Norse exactly as Tolkien's spelling is to the Norse dwarf names. Consistent philological rules are in force.

The word points toward a powerful archetype, werewolves centuries before Lon Chaney, for the word means both "wolf" and "outlaw," beast and man.

As a teenager, Tolkien entertained his friends with "horrific episodes" from *The Saga of the Volsungs* (Carpenter, 46), where Sigmund and his son Sinfjotli, living as outlaws, come in midsummer upon two princes asleep under hanging wolf skins. These skins transform the wearers into wolves, allowing them to resume human shape only every fifth day. When the heroes try on the skins, they lose human speech and shape and go on a rampage, killing eighteen men. Sigmund ultimately wounds his son in a wolfish argument, and they burn the skins (*Volsungs,* 44–45). Sigmund and Sinfjotli are literally *wargs* (wolves and outlaws), and like Tolkien's Wargs, plan deadly midsummer raids in wolf-speech, howling but understanding each other's voices. Tolkien may distinguish between wolves—a natural species that is morally neutral—and the evil Wargs when, in the Battle of Five Armies, goblin soldiers "ride upon wolves and Wargs are in their train" (236). The Wargs, boasting language and political organization, are human enough to be morally evil—"demonic"—and may be endemic werewolves, descendants of shape-changers who did not burn their skins.

Other names are derived from Germanic language but listed in the Oxford dictionary, so they are technically English, if alien to most of our vocabularies. *Orc* appears once in *The Hobbit*—in a list "goblins, hobgoblins, and orcs" (149)—and replaces *goblin* in Tolkien's other stories, probably because *goblin* carries jejune baggage from Victorian literature. The *OED* defines *orc* as "a devouring monster, an ogre" and traces it to line 112 of *Beowulf: "eotenas ond ylfe ond orc-neas,"* "giants and elves and ogres." This is a list of "evil broods" spawned by Cain's bestiality after his expulsion from the human race. (Tolkien's mythology might drop elves from the list but add Wargs.) In *The Lord of the Rings,* Tolkien derives *orc* from the Elvish word *orch* (3:409), but this is philological fiction. The word is antique English.

Arkenstone, the name for the luminous jewel that is the Heart of the Mountain, is simply a modernized spelling of Old English *earcanstan,* "precious (or holy) stone," a form of *Eorcanstanas,* which Tolkien uses to translate into Old English the word *Silmarils,* the seductive jewels that are at the heart of his Elvish history *The Silmarillion.* He had already outlined this history, parts of it in Old English, before inventing Bilbo's adventures (*Shaping,* 281). The Arkenstone is a dwarf-sized Silmaril, with the same corrupting effect on Thorin that the Silmarils had on Fëanor and his descendants. This parallel illustrates why Tolkien feared in 1938 that he had "squandered all my favorite 'motifs' and characters on the original 'Hobbit'" (*Letters,* 29).

Mirkwood, as Tolkien wrote his grandson (from memory, he says), is not his invention but "a very ancient name, weighted with legendary associations." It is a respelling of eleventh-century German *mirkiwidu,* which survived in Old English, Old Saxon, and Old Norse—the very spelling the word would have taken if it had survived in modern English. Mirkwood named the great belts of mountainous forest that were barriers to national expansion, especially between the Goths and the Huns (*Letters,* 369). Though associated with the Black Forest, the term literally means dark forest: unlit, not swarthy. Here again, Tolkien invents from philology in memorable descriptions of a forest path so dim that even dwarves, accustomed to living underground, are "sick for a sight of the sun and of the sky" (123). By good fortune (and here the *OED* confirms a grandfather's memory), the English adjective holds its ancient sense ("obscure, deficient in light"), and the Scottish or poetic spelling *mirk* is the authentic one.

Finally, there are Germanic words of marginal interest. Mount Gram uses a root meaning "fierce" in Old English and "king" in Old Norse, but buried in a burlesque passage in the uneven first chapter, a bad pun in the form of *pourquoi* myth about the origin of golf (24); and *Bard* is, of course, conventionally heroic, like the character. The names Bilbo uses to taunt the spiders of Mirkwood, though unfamiliar to readers, are all in the *OED.* What might seem wordplay in the manner of Lewis Carroll is sport of another kind: ornamental lexicography. *Attercop, Cob,* and *Lob* are rare or defunct in England, but why should they be in Tolkien's asterisk world? All mean spider. *Attercop,* the source of *cobweb,* is based on the vivid Old English compound *attorcoppa* ("poison-head"); *cob,* very rarely used, is a back-formation from *cobweb;* and *Lob,* from Old English *lobbe,* is a synonym for *spider* last documented from 1325. Finally, *Tomnoddy,* constructed like the better-known *Tom-fool,* is an insult word based on *noddy* ("fool"). "No spider," Tolkien slyly explicates, "has ever liked being called Attercop, and Tomnoddy of course is insulting to anybody." Here is flyweight philology played for humor in admittedly "not very good" verse (138), an old dictionary-writer at play.

THE ELVISH CONNECTION

Names for the blades from the troll hoard, *Orcrist* and *Glamdring,* are said to mean "Goblin-cleaver" and "Foe-hammer" in the language of Gondolin (51), an elvish stronghold that Tolkien had written about as early as 1916 (*Shaping,* 383). By then he had already invented a language for the elves with a vocabulary consciously divorced from Latin, and later in life Tolkien labored to harmonize the Elvish words from his fiction into a partial dictionary and grammar of two invented dialects. The names in *The Hobbit* were not originally part of that system, however. The story was originally "quite unconnected" to the existing mythology and languages (*Letters,* 215), and the one character who appears both in *The Hobbit* and in the Elvish chronicles, Elrond, was given that name in Bilbo's story "casually," and as a result of "the difficulty of constantly inventing good names for new characters" (*Letters,* 346). Tolkien at first did not know that Bilbo, Thorin, and Gandalf inhabited the same subcreation as his Silmarillions, a fact he "discovered" through telling the story (*Letters,* 145).

So there is reason to agree with Bob Foster ("Naming in *The Hobbit*") that Germanic and Latin roots inspired "Elvish" words in the less rigorous invention of *The Hobbit.*[9] *Orcrist,* for instance, means goblin-cleaver clearly enough if we add Old Norse *rísta* ("to cut, slash") to *orc.* Tolkien pretended, of course, that *orc* is not English, but it is. The denial is a late gesture, like a stage magician's misdirecting his audience's glance. No Germanic roots homophonic to *Glamdring* mean foe-hammer, but Old Norse *glam* ("a clash of weapons") and *drengr* ("warrior") ring true. By the same token, *Dorwinion,* a region exporting sleep-inducing fine wine, contains suspiciously the root *win* (Old English *wín,* from Latin *vinum*); and if the prefix *Dor* does not follow the correct sound-shift rules to be Old English *déore* ("precious"), then why not Latin *dormire* ("sleep") and the Latin-derived suffix *ion*? It seems too close for chance that Galion, the festive elvish butler, has a name suggesting Old English *gál* ("wanton") with the *ion* suffix, besides echoing the Latin-derived *gallant. Gondolin,* the old romanticized elf city, is helped by echoes of *gondola,* hence of Venice. And so forth.

There is some merit in what Tolkien called "unauthentic embroideries on my work" that bypass clues in his notes and appendices (*Letters,* 380). Most of the "Elvish" names, including some of the above, were indeed annotated into the fictional Elvish as part of the official "intention," but intention may be doubled or forgotten. Tolkien admits that Old English roots, for instance, seeded words later transplanted into Elvish (*Letters,* 385–86), and some place names in *The Lord of the Rings,* such as *Orthanc,* have authorized etymologies in both Elvish and Old English. His distinction between (1) the meaning of names within his fictional construction and (2) "sources in my mind, *exterior* to the story, of the forms of the names" (*Letters,* 380) allows the assumption that "Elvish" names from Latin or Old English were given fictional cover derivations in notes and stories outside *The Hobbit.* As readers are likely to sense Germanic and Latin roots through modern English vocabulary but not Elvish ones, a practice of using but hiding derivations could be effective.

Some of the Elvish names in *The Hobbit* appeared years earlier in Tolkien's unpublished histories, particularly "The Fall of Gondolin," a polished *Aeneid*-like tale of an elf-city's fall (*Lost,* 2:151–97), and others are assigned glosses within the fictional construction. Yet even as he glosses *Elrond* "Star-dome," *Moria* "The Black Chasm," and *Gondolin* "The Hidden Rock"; even as he lists Elvish roots such as *gal* ("shine") for *Galian, Glamhoth* ("Hate-host, Orc") for *Glamdring,* and *dor* ("inhabited place") for *Dorwinion*—yes, even as Tolkien authorizes fictional etymologies from Elvish dialects—he is operating within a linguistic aesthetic of modern English. Put bluntly, names still have to sound right to half-educated readers. Even as the Elvish glosses add a second layer of meaning, the names must resonate in the Latin-Germanic context of English.

There is no harm in noticing associations that color names for readers. For instance, *Bladorthin* (bladder-thin?) rings false for a respected wizard but true for a dead king (243). *Smaug,* the philological jest suggesting rebirth, really does sound like "smog," making a connection (clearer in "The Fall of Gondolin") between dragons and the monstrosities of mechanized war and industry, which Tolkien blames on goblins (60). *Warg,* with all its Germanic pedigree, sounds like a bare-toothed growl. *Gollum* and *Bolg* sound sinister, *Elrond* and *Gondolin* refined. *Roäc* and *Carc* imitate voices of the ravens. All this is an elusive matter, impossible to prove, but art that does not work in this elusive way does not work.

Some names float freely in the language aesthetic, eluding definitive etymologies after decades of efforts to tie them down. *Hobbit* itself is one of these, rationalized after the fact by an Old English asterisk word meaning "hole-dweller" (*Rings,* 2:416), but clearly (as the story of its invention on a blank page of an examination book shows) it was a product of free association. Such association can be more complex than scientific derivation, hinting of *hobgoblin, rabbit, habit, Bob, Babbit,* and similar words nearby in the language pool. The variety of suggested etymologies disqualifies any given one. The same can be said for Bilbo. It may be a nonsense name, analogous to Gorbo in *The Marvellous Land of Snergs,* which Tolkien acknowledged imitating—sloshing about with *bill, boy, Bill, bo, billet,* and *bilbo,* all in the *OED* and thus the language pool.

When he objected to a publisher's blurb comparing *The Hobbit* to *Alice's Adventures in Wonderland,* calling him "a professor of an abstruse subject at play" (*Letters,* 21), Tolkien was twenty years immersed in philology and did not realize how much it had shaped his imagination. The "only philological remark" that he identifies in the book is by no means the only tracing of his academic passion. Just as a mathematician's fascination with symbolic logic and illogic, with what does and does not follow, imbues Professor Dodgson's *Alice's Adventures in Wonderland,* so Professor Tolkien's fiction is saturated with the history of words. More than most writers, he created by naming.

Appendix: Approaches to Teaching

READING ALOUD

The Hobbit is suitable for a wide range of grades, depending on how it is presented. Begun as a bedtime story for Tolkien's three sons when they were approximately six, ten, and thirteen (though it was published years later), the story may work as the classroom equivalent of a leisurely bedtime serial in a read-aloud program. Its nineteen chapters average about thirty minutes each; and if these periods are too long, most chapters include suspenseful breaks that a teacher may find by looking ahead. Read aloud as part of a literature-based reading program, *The Hobbit* may be used as early as the first grade. Rothlein and Meinabach suggest the book for grades 1–3[1]; Saltman, in sharp contrast and presumably with silent reading in mind, suggests grades 5–8[2]; and Sutherland and Arbuthnot resolve the contradiction by observing, "No other fantasy of our time has appealed to as broad a range of readers as has *The Hobbit*."[3]

Teachers should be warned, however, that the long first chapter—probably the shakiest chapter in the book from a literary critical point-of-view anyway—is likely to weary children with short attention spans before they can be hooked on the action of later chapters. Children, even adults, may be troubled by the many ornamental dwarf names and the cute domesticity and childishness of this chapter. It is the chapter in which Tolkien made the most stylistic revisions, very nearly a false start. The teacher may wish to read the first few pages, perhaps through the first conversation with Gandalf, and then summarize the action until a few pages into the second chapter, when the dwarves are alone in the dark and send Bilbo to investigate the trolls' fire. That *The Hobbit* has succeeded despite its slow first chapter is a tribute to the energy of the rest of the story.

SILENT READING

Similarly, children reading the book silently might be reassured that they do not need to remember the dwarf names and that they may skip to the second chapter rather than putting the book down. As part of a silent reading program, reading list, or classroom library, *The Hobbit* may be phased in as early as the third grade, with no clear upward limit. A children's book that (along with its three-volume sequel) fascinated a generation of college readers cannot be declared unsuitable even for high school students, especially if it is linked with other books set in Tolkien's Middle-earth. An adult hero and maturely realized setting recommend *The Hobbit* to children of any grade with an interest in fantasy literature. Though many adult classics have become children's books, Bilbo's adventure is unusual in having moved in the opposite direction: published as a children's book, currently sold from adult shelves in stores.

A teacher may cut an inexpensive paperback edition of *The Hobbit* into separate chapters (using a razor blade or equivalent) to produce a stack of one-chapter booklets, approximately one per child. Then each child silently reads a chapter and, in sequence, tells what happens in that chapter, so that the class together narrates the whole story. The teacher may narrate chapters, of course, if fewer than nineteen children participate, or longer chapters may be subdivided. This rapid overview of the story may encourage children to read the whole story on their own.

Appendix

USING RECORDINGS

Reading aloud and silent reading may be supplemented by commercial tapes of the story. Tolkien himself reads most of the Gollum chapter on a Caedmon recording (TC 1477), and a spirited BBC radio dramatization, quite accurate and not much condensed, is available from The Minds Eye, Box 1060, Petaluma, CA 94953. The made-for-television cartoon movie version from Rankin-Bass is readily available in rental stores. The latter, however, greatly simplifies the story and imposes simplistic interpretations (an explicit antiwar message, for instance). Talking or writing about differences between two versions, which is better and why, may be a high-level cognitive exercise and an excellent occasion for language development, especially if children are encouraged to be specific.

The teacher may pause at points where Bilbo faces crucial decisions. There are many such points in the story, which is constructed almost as a series of moral tests for its hero. Children may discuss what he should do next and what the likely result will be. This might be a brief writing opportunity as well as an opportunity to discuss values and decision making. Then the teacher may read on to see what happened.

VISUAL ARTS

The Hobbit may be extended and shared by a variety of artistic approaches. A class may subdivide into groups, each taking a part of the story, for the purpose of painting a mural, either on a long roll of paper or in separate panels that, when hung together, track Bilbo's adventures from beginning to end. Similarly, a time line of the story may be written out on a roll of paper, with written references to key events, and pictures appropriate to various parts of the story taped to the roll as it is hung along a wall. Children may draw caricatures of favorite characters in the story. Tolkien drew detailed landscapes but very few detailed pictures of his characters, so readers may feel free to visualize, unhampered by any authoritative drawings.

Alternately, the teacher may read a scene, particularly one illustrated by Tolkien. After children draw their own visualizations of the text, theirs may be compared with Tolkien's—with care to allow that, though he wrote the text, his illustrations are only his visualizations, not the "right" ones. Children may discuss what Tolkien's pictures, and their own, add to the words of the story, or subtract from them. Children may draw posters, such as a missing-person poster for Bilbo, a wanted poster for Gollum, a poster recruiting an expert burglar, or a road sign warning of goblins or giant spiders. These may, of course, be hand drawn or produced on computers if desktop publishing software is available. Children, working individually or as a group, may print a mock newspaper page that turns major events from *The Hobbit* into illustrated news stories, such as "Respected Hobbit Missing," "Dragon Slain," or "Elves Blamed in Kidnapping." Peep boxes, costumes, masks, or clay sculptures are other ways to recreate characters or scenes. Children with musical interests may perform the verses said to be sung in *The Hobbit*, treating them either as traditional songs or as raps performed to rhythm instruments. The dwarves' songs seem particularly suitable for this.

LANGUAGE ARTS

A variety of group language arts activities may enlarge children's interest and understanding. After a class is familiar with the story, individual children may pretend to be characters in it—or even characters implied but not present in the story, such as a stay-at-home hobbit neighbor or a carpenter rebuilding Dale—and stage a make-believe TV talk show. The teacher or a verbally quick child may play Oprah (or Donahue) and examine issues raised by Bilbo's adventures, with questions and reactions from an "audience" of the rest of the class. The activity may be videotaped.

The essence of this simulation, which may used without the TV format, is to ask individuals to speak as characters from the story and to reflect what the characters think and know. They should omit what a character is ignorant of and represent that character's attitudes. Gollum, for instance, will mutter about the nasty little thief who invaded his home. Children should be given time to prepare and even to dress up in costume as characters.

Another dramatic simulation would be a trial in a mock courtroom: trying Bilbo, for instance, or settling the estate of Smaug. This would relate to social studies and involve learning the conduct of a legal hearing.

Included in most of the above teaching suggestions are writing opportunities if children write their responses—for instance, Smaug's version of the story, what Bilbo should do with the Arkenstone, what characters looked like, and so forth.

Several episodes are suitable for scripting and staging with a narrator, props, costumes, even sets of refrigerator boxes and whatnot. This could be a writing opportunity, with children adapting the script from the book, aided by an adult as necessary. The incident with the trolls, the encounter with the goblins and Gollum, the visit with Beorn, the encounter with the spiders and elves, and the meetings with Smaug all should work if freely staged. Larger episodes could be full class projects, or smaller episodes projects for smaller groups. Dramatizations could include choral reading or singing of Tolkien's songs or new verses written by children. Individuals might work up monologues, reading from the book or adapting by adding lines.

SOCIAL ISSUES

The absolute lack of living female characters in the story raises interesting gender issues and opportunities. The first person mentioned is Bilbo's dead mother, but subsequently there are kings without queens, town scenes without mothers or children. All creatures, including the dragon and the giant spiders, take masculine pronouns. Though many boy's books are heavily masculine—*The Wind in the Willows, King Solomon's Mines, Treasure Island,* and *Winnie-the-Pooh*, for instance— all of these have female characters, so *The Hobbit* is quite unusual, perhaps unique, in its treatment of gender. Furthermore, many of Tolkien's characters, including the hero, are generously endowed with "feminine" traits. Gandalf is as much like Baum's Good Witch Glinda as he is like Merlin; and the trolls, Gollum, Beorn, the spiders, the Elvenking, and Smaug may just as well be female. A change of pronouns, sometimes a change in costume, and the boy's book becomes a girl's book, a British *The Wizard of Oz*.

Put simply, the vacuum of females suggests that males play female roles, or that Tolkien was driven to mask the female with male pronouns. Without worrying over biographical explanations, a teacher may rework some of the class dramatizations discussed above—or diaries and other writing opportunities—with the idea of casting Bilbo, Gandalf, Gollum, Beorn, and Smaug as women and discovering how little becomes awkward or improbable. How does a female Bilbo recover her connection with her mother? How does she learn to be assertive and independent of her fairy godmother, Gandalf? Why do the traditionally masculine dwarves need her? ("She" is no Snow White, but contrasts with the dwarves as Baum's Dorothy might.) This approach may introduce girls to Tolkien's gentle sword-and-sorcery fantasy, a genre that usually appeals to boys.

Some teachers may face parental objections to teaching a fantasy that includes magic, which is associated with occultism. Tolkien's own answer to this sort of objection was complex and is summarized in chapter 4 of this book. It must suffice here to note that he distinguished morbid fantasizing from a healthy fantasy. He believed that his fiction presented positive moral lessons through symbolism. Tolkien was a devout Christian and saw his writing as a practice of devotion, but avoided imposing religious views on readers. His work is thus by design the very opposite of occultism. Anyone not satisfied by this may read Tolkien's essay "On Fairy-Stories" and the Carpenter biography, or will not be satisfied.

Notes and References

Chapter 1

1. Humphrey Carpenter, *Tolkien: A Biography* (Boston: Houghton Mifflin, 1977), 24; hereafter cited in text.

2. J. R. R. Tolkien, *Letters,* ed. Humphrey Carpenter (Boston: Houghton Mifflin, 1981), 54; hereafter cited in text as *Letters.*

3. J. R. R. Tolkien, *Tree and Leaf* (Boston: Houghton Mifflin, 1965), 79; hereafter cited in text as *Tree.*

Chapter 2

1. For more detailed accounts of the movement see Philip W. Helms, "The Evolution of Tolkien Fandom," in *The Tolkien Scrapbook,* ed. Alida Becker (New York: Grosset and Dunlap, 1974), 104–9, and Nigel Walmsley, "Tolkien and the '60s," *J. R. R. Tolkien: This Far Land,* ed. Robert Giddings (Totowa, N.J.: Barnes and Noble, 1984), 73–85.

2. Randel Helms, "Tolkien's Leaf: *The Hobbit* and the Discovery of a World," in *Tolkien's World* (Boston: Houghton Mifflin, 1974), 19–40; hereafter cited in text.

3. Edmund Wilson, "Oo, Those Awful Orcs," in *The Tolkien Scrapbook,* ed. Alida Becker, 50–55; Burton Raffel, "*The Lord of the Rings* as Literature," in *Tolkien and the Critics,* ed. Neil D. Isaacs and Rose A. Zimbardo (Notre Dame: University of Notre Dame Press, 1968), 218–46.

4. Though they make excessive claims to have discovered Tolkien's conscious sources, Robert Giddings and Elizabeth Holland in *J. R. R. Tolkien: The Shores of Middle-Earth* (Frederick, Md.: Aletheia Books, 1981) show parallels between Tolkien's stories and popular adventure fiction. Tolkien had in the theological "Father Brown" detective stories of G. K. Chesterton (1874–1936) a precedent for his use of popular forms for high purposes.

Chapter 3

1. *Current Biography Yearbook* (Bronx: H. W. Wilson, 1967), 416–17.

2. M. L. Becker, "Books for Young People," *New York Herald Tribune Books,* 20 February 1938, 7.

3. C. S. Lewis, "A World for Children," *London Times Literary Supplement,* 2 October 1937, 714.

4. Richard Hughes, "Books for Pre-Adults," *New Statesman and Nation* 4 December 1937, 944.

5. Marcus Crouch, *Treasure Seekers and Borrowers: Children's Books in Britain, 1900–1960* (London: Library Association, 1962), 67.

6. Marcus Crouch, *The Nesbit Tradition: The Children's Novel in England, 1945–1970* (London: Ernest Benn, 1972), 23.

7. Paul H. Kocher, *Master of Middle-Earth: The Fiction of J. R. R. Tolkien* (Boston: Houghton Mifflin, 1972), 19.

8. Robley Evans, *J. R. R. Tolkien* (New York: Warner, 1972), 91.

9. William H. Green, "The Four-Part Structure of Bilbo's Education," *Children's Literature* 8 (1979): 135–36.

10. Dorothy Matthews, "The Psychological Journey of Bilbo Baggins," in *A Tolkien Compass,* ed. Jared C. Lobdell (LaSalle, Ill.: Open Court, 1975), 29–42.

11. Anne C. Petty, *One Ring to Bind Them All: Tolkien's Mythology* (University: University of Alabama Press, 1979), 16.

12. Timothy R. O'Neill, *The Individuated Hobbit: Jung, Tolkien, and the Archetypes of Middle-Earth* (Boston: Houghton Mifflin, 1979), 116.

13. Richard Mathews, *Lightning from a Clear Sky: Tolkien, the Trilogy, and the Silmarillion* (San Bernardino, Calif.: Borgo, 1978), 16; hereafter cited in text.

14. Jane Chance Nitzsche, *Tolkien's Art: A "Mythology for England"* (New York: St. Martin's, 1979), 2; hereafter cited in text.

15. Lois R. Kuznets, "Tolkien and the Rhetoric of Childhood," in *Tolkien: New Critical Perspectives,* ed. Neil D. Isaacs and Rose A. Zimbardo (Lexington: University of Kentucky Press, 1981), 150; hereafter cited in text.

16. Katharyn F. Crabbe, *J. R. R. Tolkien* (New York: Frederick Ungar, 1981), 28; hereafter cited in text.

17. See Giddings and Holland, *J. R. R. Tolkien: The Shores of Middle-Earth,* and Robert Giddings, ed., *J. R. R. Tolkien: This Far Land* (London: Vision, 1983).

18. Kenneth McLeish, "The Rippingest Yarn of All," in *J. R. R. Tolkien: This Far Land,* ed. Giddings, 126–27.

19. T. A. Shippey, *The Road to Middle-Earth* (Boston: Houghton Mifflin, 1983), 61; hereafter cited in text.

Chapter 4

1. *Sir Philip Sidney's Defense of Poesy,* ed. Lewis Soens (Lincoln: University of Nebraska Press, 1979), 9.

2. I. A. Richards, *Coleridge on Imagination* (Bloomington: Indiana University Press, 1960), 167; hereafter cited in text. See *Tree,* 57–59, for Tolkien's parallel point.

3. Samuel Taylor Coleridge, *Biographia Literaria,* ed. George Watson (New York: Dutton, 1965), 168–69.

4. Edgar Allan Poe, *Poe's Poems and Essays* (New York: Dutton, 1964), 166.

Chapter 6

1. A. A. Milne, *The World of Pooh* (New York: Dutton, 1957), 297; hereafter cited in text.

2. Marie-Louise von Franz, *Shadow and Evil in Fairy Tales* (Irving, Tex.: Spring Publications, 1980), 147; hereafter cited in text.

3. Miguel de Cervantes, *The Adventures of Don Quixote,* trans. J. M. Cohen (New York: Penguin Books, 1950), 70; hereafter cited in text.

4. J. R. R. Tolkien, *Unfinished Tales of Númenor and Middle-Earth,* ed. Christopher Tolkien (New York: Ballantine, 1988), 337; hereafter cited in text as *Unfinished.*

5. Northrop Frye, *The Secular Scripture: A Study of the Structure of Romance* (Cambridge: Harvard University Press, 1976), 174; hereafter cited in text.

Chapter 7

1. Erich Neumann, *The Origins and History of Consciousness* (New York: Pantheon, 1954), 187; hereafter cited in text.

2. Lewis Carroll, *Alice in Wonderland and Through the Looking Glass* (New York: Grosset and Dunlap, 1982), 41.

3. Henry Adams Bellows, trans., *The Poetic Edda* (London: Oxford University Press, 1923), 170, 21; hereafter cited in text.

4. *Saga of the Volsungs: The Norse Epic of Sigurd the Dragon Slayer,* trans. Jesse L. Byock (Berkeley: University of California Press, 1990), 71; hereafter cited in text as *Volsungs.*

5. Lady Gregory, trans., *Gods and Fighting Men* (New York: Oxford University Press, 1970), 237–39; hereafter cited in text.

6. Erich Neumann, *The Great Mother: An Analysis of the Archetype,* trans. Ralph Manheim (Princeton: Princeton University Press, 1963) 226–32; hereafter cited in text.

7. Marie-Louise von Franz, *Introduction to the Interpretation of Fairy Tales* (Dallas: Spring Publications, 1982), 65; hereafter cited in text.

8. Jacob and Wilhelm Grimm, *The Complete Fairy Tales of the Brothers Grimm,* trans. Jack Zipes (New York: Bantam, 1987), 403–4.

9. This process, the focus of Erich Neumann's life work, is also detailed in his *The Child: Structure and Dynamics of the Nascent Personality* (London: Hodder and Stroughton, 1973); hereafter cited in text.

10. See R. W. Chambers, *Beowulf: An Introduction to the Study of the Poem* (Cambridge: Cambridge University Press, 1967), 179; hereafter cited in text.

11. *Grettir's Saga,* trans. Denton Fox and Hermann Páksson (Toronto: University of Toronto Press, 1974), 37–38; hereafter cited in text as *Grettir.*

12. *The Saga of King Heidrek the Wise,* trans. Christopher Tolkien (London: Nelson, 1960), 13–18; hereafter cited in text as *Heidrek.*

13. Georgia Dunham Kelchner, *Dreams in Old Norse Literature and Their Affinities in Folklore* (Cambridge: Cambridge University Press, 1935), 67.

14. H. Rider Haggard, *King Solomon's Mines* (New York: Oxford University Press, 1989), 85–86; hereafter cited in text.

15. Geoffrey Chaucer, *Works,* ed. F. N. Robinson, 2d ed. (Boston: Houghton Mifflin, 1957), 152.

16. J. R. R. Tolkien, *The Book of Lost Tales,* ed. Christopher Tolkien, 2 vols. (New York: Ballantine, 1992), 2:146–222; hereafter cited in text as *Book.*

17. J. R. R. Tolkien, *The Lost Road and Other Writings,* ed. Christopher Tolkien (Boston: Houghton Mifflin, 1987), 144; hereafter cited in text as *Lost.*

18. Tolkien's elves are firstborn of all the races of the earth, created before the sun and moon—in the symbology of hero and creation myths, before emergence of individual consciousness. See Neumann's *The Origins and History of Consciousness,* 6. According to the 1937 edition of *The Hobbit,* "In the Wide World the Wood-elves lingered in the twilight after the raising of the Sun and Moon; and afterwards they wandered in the forests that grew beneath the sunrise." See *The Annotated Hobbit,* ed. Douglas A. Anderson (Boston: Houghton Mifflin, 1988), 327; hereafter cited in text as *Annotated.* The elves, associated with dreams, are positive creatures of twilight consciousness, where conscious and unconscious contents merge.

19. John R. Clark Hall, trans., *Beowulf and the Finnesburg Fragment,* rev. C. L. Wrenn (London: George Allen and Unwin, 1950), 106.

20. Edward W. Said, *Beginnings: Intention and Method* (New York: Columbia University Press, 1985), 3.

Chapter 8

1. Reprinted in *The Annotated Hobbit,* 305.

2. L. Frank Baum, *The Wizard of Oz* (New York: Grosset and Dunlap, 1963), 43.

3. The Rankin-Bass film (1977) oversimplifies the story of *The Hobbit* to an antiwar stance. While Tolkien does blame Thorin for his willingness to start a needless war, to fight for the letter of selfish prerogatives, the dwarf is redeemed by dying in a just and necessary war. Tolkien dramatizes the tragedy of all wars, but only condemns unjust ones.

4. George MacDonald, *The Princess and the Goblin and The Princess and Curdie* (New York: Oxford University Press, 1990), 46; hereafter cited in text.

5. J. R. R. Tolkien, *The Shaping of Middle-Earth,* ed. Christopher Tolkien (Boston: Houghton Mifflin, 1986), 82; hereafter cited in text as *Shaping.*

6. Asked what his Elvish name was, Tolkien declined to give himself one, saying he did not belong inside his "invented history; and [did] not wish to!" See *Letters,* 398.

7. The power of the space between waking and sleeping is examined in Mary Watkins, *Waking Dreams* (Dallas: Spring, 1984).

8. H. Rider Haggard, *She,* ed. Daniel Karlin (New York: Oxford University Press), 105.

9. Daniel Defoe, *Robinson Crusoe,* ed. Michael Shinagel (New York: Norton, 1975), 39.

10. Marie-Louise von Franz, "The Process of Individuation," *Man and His Symbols,* ed. Carl G. Jung (New York: Dell, 1968), 174.

11. Bilbo's "horrible game of blind-man's-buff" with the goblin guards (81) is strongly reminiscent of several seriocomic crowd scenes in the brilliant 1933 Universal film *The Invisible Man.*

12. Helen Palmer, *The Enneagram: Understanding Yourself and the Others in Your Life* (San Francisco: Harper and Row, 1988), 204–36.

13. Snorri Sturluson, *Edda: Prologue and Gylfaginning,* ed. Anthony Faulkes (Oxford: Clarendon Press, 1982), 31; hereafter cited in text

14. *The Exeter Book,* ed. George Phillip Krapp and Elliott Van Kirk Dobbie (New York: Columbia University Press, 1936), lxvi–lxvii.

15. J. R. R. Tolkien, "Prefatory Remarks," *Beowulf and the Finnesburg Fragment,* trans. John R. Clark Hall, rev. C. L. Wrenn (London: George Allen and Unwin, 1950), xii; hereafter cited in text as "Prefatory."

16. This is elaborated in chapter 5 of my 1969 Louisiana State University dissertation, "The Hobbit and Other Fiction by J. R. R. Tolkien: Their Roots in Medieval Heroic Literature and Language," *Dissertation Abstracts International* 30 (1970): 4944A.

17. Lady Gregory, *Cuchulain of Muirthemne* (New York: Oxford University Press, 1970), 22; hereafter cited in text.

18. C. G. Jung, *Four Archetypes,* trans. R. F. C. Hull (Princeton: Princeton University Press, 1969), 79; hereafter cited in text.

19. H. G. Wells, *The Invisible Man* (New York: Bantam, 1970), 113–14.

Chapter 9

1. Marie-Louise von Franz, *Individuation in Fairy Tales* (Zurich: Spring Publications, 1977), 116.

2. While "crucified" may exaggerate, Thorin does almost kill Bilbo by dashing him onto rocks. Apparently, only a plea from Gandalf saves him (233).

3. C. G. Jung, *The Spirit in Man, Art, and Literature,* trans. R. F. C. Hull (Princeton: Princeton University Press, 1966), 87–89.

4. *The Nibelungenlied,* trans. Helen M. Mustard, in *Medieval Epics* (New York: Modern Library, 1963), 231.

5. Sir Thomas Malory, *Le Morte D'Arthur* (London: Everyman's Library, 1963), 1:44, 63.

6. Chrétien de Troyes, *Ywain, or The Knight of the Lion,* trans. Ruth Harwood Cline (Athens: University of Georgia Press, 1975), 29–35.

7. Volumes containing important pre-*Hobbit* fiction, all edited by Christopher Tolkien and published by Houghton Mifflin, are *The Book of Lost Tales 1* (1983), *The Book of Lost Tales 2* (1984), *The Shaping of Middle-Earth* (1986), and *The Lost Road and Other Writings* (1987). *The Silmarillion* (1977), a posthumous harmony of these diverse gospels, includes later revisions and differs substantially from the c. 1930 "Silmarillion" named as a source.

8. J. R. R. Tolkien, trans., *Sir Gawain and the Green Knight, Pearl, and Sir Orfeo* (Boston: Houghton Mifflin, 1975), 7; hereafter cited in text as *Orfeo.*

9. Robert D. Stevick, *Five Middle English Narratives* (New York: Bobbs-Merril, 1967), 14.

10. See book 9 of any edition of *The Odyssey.*

11. Lin Carter, *Tolkien: A Look behind The Lord of the Rings* (New York: Ballantine, 1969), 25.

Chapter 10

1. Sigurd's evasive conversation with the dying Fafnir is central to the *Fafnismol* in the *Edda* (Bellows, 372–78) and is retold with few changes in Snorri's *Prose Edda* (112) and *The Saga of the Volsungs* (63–65), adventure stories that young Tolkien found "best of all" (*Tree,* 41).

2. E. V. Gordon, ed., *An Introduction to Old Norse* (London: Oxford University Press, 1957), xxxii; hereafter cited in text.

3. In *Beowulf,* line 2405, the outlaw takes a "famous precious vessel."

4. Compare lines 2312–15 in *Beowulf* to the raid on Esgaroth in *The Hobbit* (210–12).

5. Edmund Spenser, *Edmund Spenser's Poetry,* ed. Hugh Maclean (New York: W. W. Norton, 1968), 128; hereafter cited in text.

6. Christopher Tolkien observes that "the idea of a skyrta against which all weapons are powerless is extremely common in the late sagas" (*Heidrek,* 7).

7. Chrétien de Troyes, *Arthurian Romances,* trans. W. W. Comfort (New York: Dutton, 1975), 34–35.

Chapter 11

1. In *The Lord of the Rings* most names are derived from either Elvish or Old English and its Germanic cousins. Names that are transparent in *The Hobbit* normally acquire opaque synonyms in its sequel: goblins become orcs, the Mountain becomes Erebor, and the Elvenking becomes Thranduil. Names are doubled and tripled. Gandalf is Mithrandir and Olórin; hobbits are halflings and periannath. When Aragorn conducts the hobbits through territory simply called the "Lone-lands" in *The Hobbit,* he speaks in *The Lord of the Rings* like a polyglot atlas: "We have now come to the River Hoarwell, that the Elves call Mitheithel. It flows down out of the Ettenmoors, the troll-fells north of Rivendell, and joints the Loudwater after that." See *The Lord of the Rings,* 3 vols. (Boston: Houghton Mifflin, 1965), 1:212; hereafter cited in text as *Rings.*

2. Like Tolkien, I have substituted *th* for thorn and edh, used *w* for *v,* and omitted the inflectional *n* and *r.* Names found in *The Hobbit* are italicized.

3. *Elder or Poetic Edda,* ed. and trans. Olive Bray (London: Viking Club, 1908), 280.

4. Christopher Tolkien, "Foreword," to J. R. R. Tolkien, *The Hobbit* (Boston: Houghton Mifflin, 1987), iii.

5. *Beowulf and the Fight at Finnsburg,* ed. Fr. Klaeber, 3d ed. (Boston: D. C. Heath, 1950), xxv–xxvi.

6. Snorri Sturluson, *Heimskringla: The Olaf Sagas,* trans. Samuel Laing (London: Dutton, 1964), 5–6.

7. Stuart Robertson and Frederic G. Cassidy, *The Development of Modern English,* 2d ed. (Englewood Cliffs, N.J.: Prentice-Hall, 1954), 253–55.

8. J. S. Ryan, "Germanic Mythology Applied—The Extension of the Literary Folk Memory," *Folklore* 77 (1966): 54–59.

9. Bob Foster, "Naming in *The Hobbit,*" *Mythprint,* November 1975, 2–3.

Appendix

1. Liz Rothlein and Anita Meyer Meinbach, *The Literature Connection: Using Children's Books in the Classroom* (Glenview, Ill.: Scott, Foresman, 1991), 19.

2. Judith Saltman, *The Riverside Anthology of Children's Literature,* 6th ed. (Boston: Houghton Mifflin, 1985), 1266.

3. Zena Sutherland and Mary Hill Arbuthnot, *Children and Books* (New York: HarperCollins, 1991), 252.

Selected Bibliography

Primary Works

The Annotated Hobbit. Introduction and notes by Douglas A. Anderson. Boston: Houghton Mifflin, 1988. The 1966 text of *The Hobbit* with notes and illustrations in the margins. Includes useful work with sources, a publication history, and an appendix detailing textual revisions made by Tolkien.

The Book of Lost Tales. 2 vols. Edited by Christopher Tolkien. Boston: Houghton Mifflin, 1983. Paperback by Ballantine Books, 1992. Tolkien's earliest tales include "The Fall of Gondolin," a source of *The Hobbit*'s mythical history.

The Hobbit, or There and Back Again. Boston: Houghton Mifflin, 1938. The first American edition with the original text of chapters 1 and 4, later much revised.

The Hobbit, or There and Back Again. Boston: Houghton Mifflin, 1966. A high-quality edition incorporating Tolkien's final revisions (more cheaply printed by Ballantine Books, New York, 1966). Houghton Mifflin has also printed hardbound deluxe editions, including a fiftieth anniversary reprint with foreword by Christopher Tolkien.

The Letters. Edited by Humphrey Carpenter. Boston: Houghton Mifflin, 1981. An invaluable guide to Tolkien's writing methodology and his strong, unusual character and values.

The Lord of the Rings. 3 vols. 2d ed. Boston: Houghton Mifflin, 1965. Revision of the 1954–55 adult sequel to *The Hobbit*. Available as a Ballantine paperback (1965).

The Lost Road and Other Writings. Edited by Christopher Tolkien. Boston: Houghton Mifflin, 1987. An incomplete novel and mythological manuscripts from the period of the completion and publication of *The Hobbit.*

"On Fairy-Stories." In *Essays Presented to Charles Williams,* edited by C. S. Lewis, 38–89. London: Oxford University Press, 1947; Grand Rapids, Mich.: William B. Eerdmans, 1966. Revised and reprinted in *Tree and Leaf.* Boston: Houghton Mifflin, 1965. Also reprinted in *The Tolkien Reader.* New York: Ballantine, 1966, 1975. A major critical text defending the seriousness of fantasy and constructing a theory applicable to all of Tolkien's fiction.

"Prefatory Remarks." *Beowulf and the Finnesburg Fragment.* Translated by John R. Clark Hall. Revised by C. L. Wrenn. London: George Allen and Unwin, 1940. Remarks written after the publication of *The Hobbit* give direct insight into names and riddles, Old English elements in the story. Hall's translation is useful for readers wishing to explore the *Beowulf* connection.

The Shaping of Middle-Earth. Edited by Christopher Tolkien. Boston: Houghton Mifflin, 1986. Mythological manuscripts from the period of the composition of *The Hobbit,* including the "Silmarillion," which Tolkien credits as a source.

The Silmarillion. Edited by Christopher Tolkien. Boston: Houghton Mifflin, 1977. The best-selling posthumous compilation of Tolkien's final intentions for his Elvish history, different at many points from earlier texts that influenced *The Hobbit.*

Sir Gawain and the Green Knight, Pearl, and Sir Orfeo. Translated by J. R. R. Tolkien. Boston: Houghton Mifflin, 1975. The last poem directly influenced his treatment of Bilbo and the Wood-elves.

Unfinished Tales of Númenor and Middle-Earth. Edited by Christopher Tolkien. Boston: Houghton Mifflin, 1980. Paperback by Ballantine Books, 1988. Narrative fragments of background to his fiction, including a retelling of events in *The Hobbit* in Gandalf's voice.

Secondary Works

Becker, Alida, ed. *The Tolkien Scrapbook.* New York: Grosset and Dunlap, 1974. A collection of articles from the height of the Tolkien craze, recording the enthusiasm and hostility of the time.

Carpenter, Humphrey. *Tolkien: A Biography.* Boston: Houghton Mifflin, 1977. A lucid and fascinating authorized biography of the artist.

Chrétien de Troyes. *Ywain, or The Knight of the Lion.* Translated by Ruth

Harwood Cline. Athens: University of Georgia Press, 1975. A medieval ring of invisibility in a cluster of other analogues.

Crabbe, Katharyn F. *J. R. R. Tolkien.* New York: Frederick Ungar, 1981. Includes an extensive chapter analyzing *The Hobbit* in structural and thematic terms.

Crouch, Marcus. *The Nesbit Tradition: The Children's Novel in England, 1945–1970.* London: Ernest Benn, 1972. Awards *The Hobbit* an honored place, with E. Nesbit, in literary history.

_____. *Treasure Seekers and Borrowers: Children's Books in Britain, 1900–1960.* London: The Library Association, 1962. Applauds *The Hobbit* in a critical history insisting on quality children's fiction.

Evans, Robley. *J. R. R. Tolkien.* New York: Warner, 1972. Discusses *The Hobbit* as if part of *The Lord of the Rings,* indirectly shows Tolkien's success in merging two originally inconsistent works.

Frye, Northrop. *The Secular Scripture: A Study of the Structure of Romance.* Cambridge: Harvard University Press, 1976. *The Hobbit* is a romance, and many of Frye's observations about the genre and its ritual or mythic functions apply to Tolkien's work.

Giddings, Robert, ed. *J. R. R. Tolkien: This Far Land.* London: Vision, 1983. A series of strong, irreverent readings outside typical academic channels, fandom turned delightfully sour, often relevant to *The Hobbit.*

Grahame, Kenneth. *The Wind in the Willows.* New York: Longmeadow Press, 1987. Reprint of the 1908 classic that the first chapters of *The Hobbit* (particularly Bilbo's home) suggest.

Green, William H. "The Four-Part Structure of Bilbo's Education." *Children's Literature* 8 (1979): 133–40. About the patterns of Bilbo's maturation.

Grettir's Saga. Translated by Denton Fox and Hermann Pálsson. Toronto: University of Toronto Press, 1974. A saga of trolls, berserks, and narrow escapes suggesting *Beowulf* and *The Hobbit.*

Haggard, H. Rider. *King Solomon's Mines.* New York: Oxford University Press, 1989. The great 1885 landlocked emulation of *Treasure Island* shares dozens of structural and descriptive motifs with *The Hobbit.*

Helms, Randell. *Tolkien's World.* Boston: Houghton Mifflin, 1974. Stimulating reading of *The Hobbit* in two chapters, seeing it as a breakthrough work and the structural prototype for its sequel.

Jung, C. G. *The Spirit of Man, Art, and Literature.* Translated by R. F. C. Hull. Princeton: Princeton University Press, 1966. The great analyst discusses the psychology of literary creation.

_____. *Four Archetypes: Mother, Rebirth, Spirit, Trickster.* Translated by R. F. C. Hull. Princeton: Princeton University Press, 1969. Four dense and masterful essays never far from themes developed in *The Hobbit.*

Kocher, Paul H. *Master of Middle-Earth: The Fiction of J. R. R. Tolkien.* Boston: Houghton Mifflin, 1972. The value of the *Hobbit* chapter is to record why those who dislike the book dislike it.

Kuznets, Lois R. "Tolkien and the Rhetoric of Childhood." In *Tolkien: New Critical Perspectives,* edited by Neil D. Isaacs and Rose A. Zimbardo, 150–62. Lexington: University of Kentucky Press, 1981. Praises *The Hobbit* for extending the tradition of great British children's books.

MacDonald, George. *The Princess and the Goblin and The Princess and Curdie.* New York: Oxford University Press, 1990. The first is an admitted source of Tolkien's goblins and tunnels.

Mathews, Richard. *Lightning from a Clear Sky: Tolkien, the Trilogy, and the Silmarillion.* San Bernardino: Borgo, 1978. A flawed study, yet makes a stimulating set of comments on *The Hobbit.*

Matthews, Dorothy. "The Psychological Journey of Bilbo Baggins." In *A Tolkien Compass,* edited by Jared C. Lobdell, 29–42. LaSalle, Ill.: Open Court, 1976. Analyzes Bilbo's process of maturation with help from Jung.

Milne, A. A. *The World of Pooh.* New York: Dutton, 1957. Reprint of classic tales (1926 and 1928) from the tradition where *The Hobbit* began, before it found heroic roots.

Nesbit, Edith. *The Story of the Amulet.* New York: Looking Glass Library, n.d. Library reprint of a turn-of-the-century adventure like *The Hobbit* in tone and pacing, with a strong presence of historical scholarship made reader-friendly.

Neumann, Erich. *The Great Mother: An Analysis of the Archetype.* 2d ed. Translated by Ralph Manheim. Princeton: Princeton University Press, 1963. A classic compendium of symbols of the positive and negative mother in art and myth.

_____. *The Origins and History of Consciousness.* Translated by R. F. C. Hull. Princeton: Princeton University Press, 1954. Analysis of the dragon-slaying hero as a symbol of growing consciousness, introduced by C. G. Jung.

Nitzsche, Jane Chance. *Tolkien's Art: A "Mythology for England."* New York: St. Martin's, 1979. Builds on Tolkien's writings as a medievalist to construct a serious structural and thematic interpretation, narrowly focused by the chosen methodology.

O'Neill, Timothy R. *The Individuated Hobbit: Jung, Tolkien, and the Archetypes of Middle-Earth.* Boston: Houghton Mifflin, 1979. Spread thin by its commitment to cover all Tolkien, still makes valuable psychological comments on *The Hobbit.*

Petty, Anne C. *One Ring to Bind Them All: Tolkien's Mythology.* University: University of Alabama Press, 1979. Rigorous structuralist analysis of *The Hobbit* and its sequel as traditional form.

Poetic Edda. Translated by Henry Adams Bellows. London: Humphrey Milford, 1923. The most ancient record of Norse mythology, including dwarves, question contests, and dragons. See also *The Elder or Poetic Edda.* 2 vols. Translated by Olive Bray. London: Viking Club, 1908. Reprint. New York: AMS Press, 1982. Patricia Terry's *Poems of the Vikings: The Elder Edda* (New York: Bobbs-Merrill, 1969) omits the passage of dwarf names.

Richards, I. A. *Coleridge on Imagination.* Bloomington: Indiana University Press, 1960. Reprint of authoritative 1934 slant on Coleridge, which Tolkien reacted against to defend fantasy.

Saga of the Volsungs: The Norse Epic of Sigurd the Dragon Slayer. Translated by Jesse L. Byock. Berkeley: University of California Press, 1990. The classic Norse dragon, with skin changers and talking birds.

Shippey, T. A. *The Road to Middle-Earth.* Boston: Houghton Mifflin, 1983. Definitive study of Tolkien's fiction in the context of his academic field, with significant insights into *The Hobbit.*

Snorri Sturluson. *The Prose Edda: Tales from Norse Mythology.* Translated by Jean I. Young. Berkeley: University of California Press, 1966. A source of the dwarf names and other influences.

von Franz, Marie-Louise. *The Feminine in Fairy Tales.* Rev. ed. Dallas: Spring, 1976. This book and the three following are lecture transcriptions, loose but helpful in applying Jungian dream interpretation and developmental psychology to fantasy fiction.

_____. *Individuation in Fairy Tales.* Dallas: Spring, 1977.

_____. *An Introduction to the Interpretation of Fairy Tales.* Rev. ed. Dallas: Spring, 1982.

_____. *Shadow and Evil in Fairy Tales.* Rev. ed. Dallas: Spring, 1980.

Wells, H. G. *The Invisible Man.* New York: Bantam, 1970. The 1897 precursor to the invisible Mr. Baggins.

Index

Index

Galion, 122

Gandalf, 41–42, 46–49, 55–56, 58, 63–67, 74, 80, 83, 101, 102, 108, 112

García Márquez, Gabriel, 10

Giddings, Robert, 18

Gilgamesh, 73

Glamdring, 121

Glinda, 67

goblins, 63–64, 69–73, 119

Goethe, Johann Wolfgang von, 8–9

Gollum, 39, 50, 64, 72, 74–76, 78–79

Gondolin, 59–61, 122

Gordon, E. V., 101, 111, 114, 116

Gottfried von Strassburg, 102

Grahame, Kenneth, 6, 17, 38

Grettir's Saga, 56, 94

Grimm Brothers (Jacob and Wilhelm), 6, 48, 52, 67

Grimm, Jacob, 114

Haggard, H. Rider, 6, 10, 18, 42, 58–59, 74, 105–6

Hall, John R. Clark, 113

Heimskringla (Snorri), 115

Helms, Randel, 10

Hesse, Hermann, 8

Hitler, 72, 76, 81

hobbit, derivation of word, 123

Holland, Elizabeth, 18

Homely Houses, 15, 44, 57–59, 65, 95–96

Homer, 52, 92, 98, 106

Hrothgar, 60–61

hubris, 49

Hughes, Richard, 12

Iliad (Homer), 106

individuation, 32–33, 80, 88–90, 100

Inferno (Dante), 69, 72

inflation of ego, 81, 97, 100

Invisible Man, The (Wells), 75, 81, 91, 107

Journey to the Center of the Earth (Verne), 74

Joyce, James, 5

Jung, C. G., 15, 30–34, 50, 74–75, 80, 88, 93, 97

Kafka, Franz, 5

Kant, Immanuel, 24

Keats, John, 92

kennings, 78

keys, symbolism of, 52, 54, 56, 84

King Solomon's Mines (Haggard), 6, 18, 58, 74, 86, 105–7

Klaeber, Fr., 114

Kocher, Paul H., 13

Koresh, David, 81

Kuznets, Lois R., 17

"La Belle Dame Sans Merci" (Keats), 92

Lang, Andrew, 6, 22, 111

Lawrence, D. H., 71

Le Morte d'Arthur (Malory), 104

Leeds University, 4, 111

Lewis, C. S., 11–12, 13, 18

Lilith (MacDonald), 99

MacDonald, George, 6, 17, 67, 69–71, 74

macho behavior, 50, 68

McLeish, Kenneth, 18

magical realism, 10, 25

Malory, Sir Thomas, 91, 104

Marvelous Land of Snergs, The (Smith), 6, 67, 123

Mathews, Richard, 16

Matthews, Dorothy, 15

maturation, 14–15, 17

Meinbach, Anita Meyer, 125

Merlin, 67

The Author

William H. Green teaches at Western Kentucky University. He received his B.A. in English from Auburn University and his Ph.D. in English, with a language minor, from Louisiana State University. His dissertation dealt with the medieval background of *The Hobbit*, and he has published Tolkien studies in *Children's Literature* and *Mythlore*. He has published more than a hundred poems and stories in various journals, including *Chicago Review, Southern Review, Mudfish, Arc, Riverside Quarterly,* and *Fantasy Macabre*, and a 1993 book of surrealist poetry, *Under the Threshold*. He has received state and local awards for research in the history of Russell County, Alabama, and for research on a local slave bridge builder about whom he has written a novel.

Demo

Demo

Demo